Tell It Like It Can Be

Tell It Like It Can Be

James R. McCormick

2019

Contents

Dedication

This book is dedicated to the memory of my parents, Martin and Vada McCormick, from whom I first heard the Good News, and in whose lives I have seen and experienced so much of God.

And to dear friends in two Sunday School Classes which I have been privileged to teach numerous times through the years, and for whom I have facilitated several retreats: the Christians Under Construction Class of First United Methodist Church of Roswell, Georgia, and the Fellowship Class of Big Canoe Chapel, Big Canoe, Georgia.

Acknowledgments

I want to express my deep appreciation to my friends, George Martin, who produced this volume, and to Patricia Irvin, for her typing and editing skills. These two have provided encouragement and support essential to the publication of this book.

Introduction

Jim has been my pastor, mentor, and colleague. Most of all he has been, and is, my friend. He helped shape my ministry, equipping, encouraging, and empowering me.

Jim has a true gift for preaching and teaching. I knew that from our first working together more than forty-five years ago. The years have not diminished it. Ours is a world hungry for *"something more."* Our dominant paradigm too often is fear and despair. We let our differences divide, and fail to see or receive the blessings in them. Jim's words speak to that world. They offer a message of undeniable hope, love, and unconditional grace.

Jim views life through the lens of the gospel. He names what is and also offers a vision of what, by the grace and power of God, can be. His writing, like his preaching, is pastoral, passionate, and prophetic. It comforts, confronts, and challenges. It's grounded in his deep faith and in the teachings and truth of Jesus. He shares himself with honesty, authenticity and integrity. He shares his faith boldly with courage and conviction.

For Jim, it's all about relationship – with the God we see in Jesus Christ, with others, with ourselves, and with the world. Jim understands the joy and pain, the struggle and the triumph, the gift and the burden of living together in love. He calls us to let that love be the guide, the center, and the direction of our lives.

Jim's books are part of his legacy. It's one I'm glad to celebrate. I'm grateful that Jim has been part of my journey and even more grateful to have been part of his.

Thank you, Jim. May your words take root in many hearts.

The Rev. Dr. Faith J. Conklin
Distinguished Pastor-in-Residence
Claremont School of Theology

Tell It Like It Can Be!

Matthew 16:13-19

In one of the "Peanuts" cartoon strips, Charlie Brown is pictured leaning against a stone wall, dejectedly holding his head in his hands. Lucy comes along and says, "Discouraged again, eh Charlie Brown? You know what your trouble is? The whole trouble with you is that you're YOU!" He looks at Lucy and says, "Well, what in the world can I do about that?" Lucy shrugs her shoulder and says, "I don't pretend to be able to give advice...I merely point out the trouble."

I.

When I saw that cartoon, after I had finished my chuckle, I thought to myself, "That's a sign of our time." We are very good at identifying problems (and there is an abundance of problems to identify), but we are not very good at finding solutions to the most basic human struggles. And, sad to say, a great many of us no longer believe that there are solutions to be found.

We pride ourselves in being a generation of realists. Our motto is, "Tell it like it is!" Idealism, optimism, belief in the future – such Pollyanna approaches to life are decidedly out of style. We want no self-delusion. We want the truth, no

13

matter how sordid or painful. We insist upon telling it like it is.

So, in recent years we have been deluged with literature, art, films and philosophy which purport to reflect life as it is. We are constantly exposed to violence, greed, exploitive sex, despair and meaninglessness. We have seen few happy endings depicted. We have seen little altruism in evidence. Noble, idealistic, loving people have been portrayed as half-mad, out of touch with the real world, like some admirable but tragic Don Quixote tilting at windmills. We may smile patronizingly at such nobility, but we realists know that you can't live like that in our kind of world. We want to tell it like it is.

And that is good, if we can in fact look at life – all of life and see it as it is. In fact, that's essential. No person can go where he wants or needs to go unless he first knows where he is. So, I do believe in realism. But I don't believe in that so-called realism which sees only the sordid, negative, despairing, hopeless side of life. All of that is a dimension of reality, but that's not all that is real. At the same time, I don't believe in that purported realism which looks at the world through rose-colored glasses and sees only the bright, cheerful, happy, positive side of life. All of that is real, too, but it is not the whole picture. I want to tell it like it is, but I want to tell all that is. I want us to see all of life, in both its positive and negative dimensions. I agree that it is important to tell it like it is, if we can tell it like it really is!

II.

But, as important as that is, there is something more important. Because of who we are, Christians are not content simply to announce present reality. We try to tell it like it is, but the thing we get excited about is telling it like it can be.

Christians are future oriented people. We believe that the future is open with limitless possibilities. The future does not have to be a carbon copy of the past or the present. It can be new!

The trouble is that a great many people don't believe that. I regret to say that most nominal Christians don't even believe that. So many people believe that the way things are is the way things will be. They don't really believe in the possibility of change for the good.

They don't believe that people can change. They are fond of clichés such as, "You can't teach an old dog new tricks." Or, "A leopard never changes his spots." That's the way they think, so that's the way they tend to act.

Without a doubt, the one thing that inhibits the solution of marriage problems more than any other is that people insist upon seeing the future in terms of the past. They are reluctant to work for a new future because they simply can't believe that the future can be any different than the past.

The one question I hear again and again in counseling is: "Do you believe that people can change? Do you believe that the future can be different than the past?" When I hear such a question I always smile and reply that if I didn't believe that, I would be out of business. The answer should be obvious to Christians. That is the business of the Church. Our primary purpose is to exchange old lives for new! And if we ever cease believing in the possibility of that, we should be honest, close our doors, and go out of business!

Tragically, not only do most people refuse to believe that others can change, they also don't believe that they can change. No matter what we say, we seem to believe that however we are, that's the way we will be. Agnes Rogers Allen wrote about that in a humorous vein by saying:

> "I should be better, brighter, thinner,
> And more intelligent at dinner.
> I should reform and take some pains,
> Improve my person, use my brains.
> There's lots that I could do about it,
> But will I? …Honestly, I doubt it."

It should come as no surprise that so many people are discouraged, defeated, despairing. They believe that the way it is, is the way it will always be. If they made a mistake, they will never recover from it. If they have missed an opportunity, they will never have another. If there is a broken relationship, it will never be healed. If there has been a failure, there will never be a success. Don't you see how deadly it can be if we insist upon seeing the future only in terms of the past? If I didn't believe in the possibility of newness, if I didn't believe that God is at work in His world to create a future that is better than the past, I could become very discouraged. Despair would come easily.

That is one reason I like the story of Jesus and Simon Peter. You will remember that before meeting Jesus, Simon had been an unknown fisherman in Galilee. He was a coarse, rough, hard-working, undistinguished fisherman. And there was no reason to believe that he would ever be anything other than that. Then Jesus came along and invited him to be His disciple. Simon followed Jesus and he began to grow. But he was still impetuous and crude and short tempered. Sometimes he was weak and faithless. Hardly the sort of material you and I would choose to fashion into a saint! But Jesus had a way of seeing things that we overlook. He helped people to see themselves as they were, that's true. But that, alone, was never enough. He also helped people to see their future possibilities. To Simon, the fisherman, He said, "Follow me and I will make you a fisher of men." To Simon, the disciple, He said, "You are Peter, the rock, and on this rock I will build my Church, and the gates of hell will not prevail against it!" Jesus was speaking at that moment not only about present reality, but about future possibility. He was not only telling it like it is, but also like it can be!

Peter took up Jesus' vision of the future. He began to believe in it. And, by the grace of God, the more he saw himself to be Peter, the rock, the more he became Peter, the rock. The scriptures remind us that, "as a person thinks in his heart, so shall he be." Do you see, then, why it is so important to tell it like it can be? Our vision of the future has a way of becoming reality! I believe that there is hope in that. There is motivation in that. There is strength in that. What everyone needs is to believe that, under God, the future can be better than the past and the present.

III.

And, at least in part, that is the good news of the Christian faith. The future is not a slave of the past nor the present. Positive change is possible, not because of our goodness, ability or hard work, but because God is at work in His world in behalf of good. God is in the business of building new futures. He works constantly at the task of constructing more authentic human beings. I have no doubt that God will make the future good for all of us if we give Him half a chance.

But we have got to begin believing that a new future is possible! I say again, that our vision of the future goes a long way in shaping that future. Do you remember the verse:

17

"Two men looked out of prison bars,
The one saw mud, the other stars."

Is there any doubt in your mind which one had the brighter future?

Examine closely the full sweep of human history and you will discover that the creative people, the innovative people were those who refused to see the future in terms of the past. The pioneers of progress have been those people who have been motivated by a vision of what could be. Whether we are talking about Socrates or Copernicus or Columbus or Pasteur or Einstein or Jesus, they all had one thing in common; they all saw the future as being different from the past. They saw the future in terms of hopeful possibility! There is a poem that says it:

"For man is dreaming ever,"
He glimpses the hills afar,"
And plans for the things out yonder
Where all his tomorrows are,
And back of the sound of the hammer,
And back of the hissing stream,
And back of the hand on the throttle,
Is ever a daring dream."

When you think about it, you will realize that that is one dimension of the grandeur of mankind. We can dream! We can imagine something that is not yet reality. William Haslitt sounded a profound note when he said, "Man is the only animal that laughs and weeps; for he is the only animal that is struck by the difference between what things are and what they ought to be."

Don't you see, it is only when we are aware of that difference between what things are and what they ought to be that we can then move in the direction of making things what they ought to be.

That is one reason the Christian faith is important. In Christ, God shows us the possibilities of the future. He calls us to become all that we are capable of becoming. He inspires us to shape His world to His intended purpose. He makes us restless and dissatisfied until we realize our potential for life. I tell you, that's a purpose big enough to live for! That is something I can become excited about!

That, then, is where the Christian life is lived — in that place of tension between where we are and where God calls us to be. I've heard Bishop Gerald Kennedy talk about it a number of times. He called it the "gap between Dorothy and Chopin." I suppose Dorothy was the little girl next door endlessly practicing her piano lessons. There were so many sour notes and dissonant chords. The gap between Dorothy and Chopin was painfully obvious. Perhaps Dorothy will never become a Chopin. That's o.k. Her task is to become the best Dorothy possible. And, in the meanwhile, grace enables her to live with whatever gap continues to exist. But isn't it clear that by reaching for the highest possible standard, Dorothy will become more than she has ever been?

I don't know about you, but I need that. I need what Whitehead called, "the habitual vision of greatness." If all you can do for me is to remind me of the way things are, I will probably become discouraged and perhaps even stop trying. But if you will constantly help me to see the way things can be, and if you will assure me that God is at work to shape a new and better future, then that will inspire me and motivate me and call forth the best from within me!

That is one of the things I appreciated about Dr. Martin Luther King. He told it like it is, to be sure. He talked about racism and injustice. He refused to put a sugar coating on the harsh realities of life. He was murdered in large measure because he insisted upon telling it like it is. But that is not all he did. And if it had been all he did – if he had been content to point out our ills, lament them and say, "That's the way things are!" he would never have achieved greatness. His influence would have been short lived. But he did more than tell it like it is. He also told it like it can be. He said, "I have a dream… I have a dream!" He planted a vision in the hearts and minds of a generation of Americans and today the future is being shaped by the vision which he helped to plant.

That is the way Jesus worked. He had no illusions about the weakness, the fickleness, the sinfulness of people like us. He saw all that in people. But that is not all He saw. He saw in every person the image of God. He saw the person they could become. He saw the gifts they had to give. And, by believing in them, Jesus helped people to become more than they ever dreamed they could be.

If we will read the Bible with our eyes wide open, we will discover that the people portrayed there are not plaster saints. They are people remarkably like us, and many of them started out far worse than us. I sometimes think that God takes disreputable people and makes them into great people just to prove what He can do with unlikely material. Think about it; Moses had been a murderer. David an adulterer. Zacchaeus a hated tax collector, Simon Peter a liar and a coward. But, by the grace of God, they all became more than they were.

Do you hear it? Jesus tells it like it can be. He gives us a vision of greatness and inspires us to move toward it. As one writer put it, "He wakes in you desires you never can forget." The good news is that in the company of Jesus you see things you never saw before. You believe things you never believed before. You become more than you have ever been before!

That has been the testimony of Christians for over 2000 years now. Once you come face to face with Jesus Christ, you change. You can't keep on doing business as usual.

I believe that Jesus has a distinctive name for each of us like the name He gave to Simon. And that name conveys a word of newness, a word of possibility for the future. "You are Peter, the rock, and on this rock I will build my Church." Remember, that up to that moment, Peter had not acted very much like a rock. But Jesus gave him a new vision of who he could be, and sustained and motivated by that vision, Peter is who he became. Thank God, Jesus not only tells it like it is, He also tells it like it can be! And that is good news!

Recently I have been reading the autobiography of the late Dr. Charles Allen. He preached his first sermon at the age of nineteen, and he was frightened to death! Almost everyone in town was there to hear the new preacher and the church was full. He preached about the prodigal son. He said that he told the people everything he knew about the prodigal, about his elder brother, and about the father. Then he told them everything else he knew about religion and about the church. When he finished that sermon he had exhausted his resources and the sermon had lasted only thirteen minutes.

He said that as they sang the last hymn, he realized that he had been a failure. He felt that preaching was not for him and that he was going home that afternoon and they could get another preacher. He was going to call the Bishop and resign right then and there. In all probability, Dr. Allen's ministry would have ended that day, but for the influence of one man.

Dr. George Washington Burnett, a man over eighty years old, had been practicing medicine in that town for more than fifty years. He was a large, impressive looking man with long white hair. He was the most influential man in the church and in the community. During the worship service that Sunday morning, Dr. Burnett sat in the front pew. When the service was over, Charles Allen tried to avoid him because he knew he would have something harsh to say about his sermon.

The doctor remained in his pew until most of the other people had gone. Then he got up and walked over to the young minister. He put his arm around him and said, "Charles, you helped me this morning. You are going home and eat dinner with me." Charles Allen went home with the doctor and his wife. During dinner the doctor talked about what a wonderful thing it is for a young man to enter the ministry and how he can help so many people. He talked about how happy he was that Charles was a minister, and that he loved him and wanted to help him.

When Charles Allen left the doctor's house that day, he felt like he was ten feet tall, and of course he had no thought of quitting. In retrospect, it was not much of a sermon. And, at that point in his life, Charles Allen was not much of a preacher. But a great man by the name of Dr. George Washington Burnett not only saw what was, he also saw what could be! Charles Allen went on to publish numerous best selling books and to become pastor of his denomination's largest congregation.

That is the way God works. God looks at our lives and, thank God, He is not content to tell it like it is. He tells it like it can be. And once we take hold of that vision... once we take hold of that vision, then, by the grace of God, we are never again the same!

Prayer: Father, we are so very grateful that you love us as we are, because we need that. But we are also grateful that you love us enough to call us to become all that we can be. We need that, too. Help us now to see the good future that You want to give us. May we be receptive to the work of Your Spirit in our lives. In the Master's name we pray. Amen.

The Main Thing

Matthew 22:35-40

We don't know what prompted the question put to Jesus that day. Mark's gospel presents the questioner as a sincere seeker after truth, but Matthew was more suspicious. People followed Jesus around every day, some as earnest seekers, but some asking questions trying to trip him up, get him into trouble. For serious Jews, no part of the law was supposed to be more important than any other part, so maybe in asking this question this man was being a troublemaker. We just don't know. What we do know is that Jesus' answer to his question is among the most important in all the pages of scripture.

"Which commandment is the greatest?" the man asked. Jesus said, "'You shall love the Lord your God with all your heart, and with all your soul, and with all your mind.' This is the first and greatest commandment. And a second is like it, 'You shall love your neighbor as yourself.'" Then He added, "On these two commandments hang all the law and the prophets." Jesus was saying that these two commandments summarize the whole Bible! The Hebrew Bible, what we often call the Old Testament, contains three parts: the law, the prophets, and the writings. In Jesus' time, the law and the prophets were the two sections that were considered scripture – the writings were added later. So, Jesus was insisting that these two commandments summed up his Bible!

Of course, Jesus was assuming something that is prior and essential, something that we cannot take for granted, but must affirm again and again. Everything starts with God's love for us! God loves us with a love that is unconditional and without limit. It is a love that is greater than our ability to put into words. God's love for us is expressed in so many gracious ways, love which we see and receive especially in God's gift of Jesus. Everything good in life starts there. When Jesus tells us that we are to love God, ourselves and others, it is clear that we are able to do all of that only because God first loves us! When we receive God's love in faith, it is only then that we are able to respond to that love by loving God with our whole being, by loving ourselves in a healthy, life-giving way, and then passing that love along by loving others without limit.

When we understand it, that is what life is all about. Life is about relationships, and life is either good or less than good depending upon the quality of those relationships. Everything else is largely context. I once worked with a youth director who was a delightful person. Carol Smith was alive to life, and she loved every teenager in her group and they loved her back, devotedly. She had a number of insightful, beautiful posters on the walls of her office. I have never forgotten one of them. It said: "The main thing in life is to make the main thing the main thing!" Think about that. According to Jesus, this is the main thing in life: relationships with God, with ourselves, and with others. And if you want your life to be good, if you want your life to be fulfilled, if you want your life to count for something special, start there, with right relationships, because that's the main thing!

When Jesus said that we are to love God, He was quoting from the sixth chapter of Deuteronomy, probably the most important passage in the Hebrew Bible. Remember, the Jewish people were the first monotheists in the history of the world. All other religions were polytheistic, believing in many gods, but not Judaism! The passage from Deuteronomy begins, "Shema Yisrael! (That's the imperative form of the verb, to hear!) Hear O Israel, the Lord our God, the Lord is one!" That affirmation sounded in the ancient world like the sound of a mighty trumpet: One God! Only one God! The passage continues, "You shall love the Lord your God with all your heart, and with all your soul, and with all your might." In other words, our love for God must be with our whole being. Our relationship with God must not be simply a pleasant additive to life, a desirable extra, something tacked on to the periphery. No! It must be at the center. It must be what life is all about. We are to love God with all we are and with all we have. We are to love God with all our being!

I'm fascinated by the fact that when Jesus quoted this passage from Deuteronomy, He added something to it. Have you ever noticed that Jesus added that, in addition to loving God with all out heart and with all our soul, we are also to love God with all our mind? Jesus added that and I like it. Those who know me well know that I am tempted to dwell on this emphasis for a time. Our faith does not ask us to put aside our minds, to park our brains outside the church before we come inside. There is no needed battle between faith and reason. Faith may be supra-rational at times, but it must never be irrational. No, we are to love God with all our mind, Jesus said. I like that, but we must move on to other parts of the scripture.

What does it mean to love God with all our being? When the Bible speaks of love, it is always more than sentiment, more than feelings. Biblical love is always more than that.

When I officiate at services of marriage, I always point out that while good feelings are nice and desirable when they are present, the reality is that feelings are undependable and uncontrollable. There must be more to love than, "I feel good about you in this moment." No, lasting love must go beyond feelings to commitment. It must involve a decision about how we're going to act, no matter how we may feel in a given moment. So, our love for God must go beyond feelings. It must be an act of the will. It must be about what we value above all else, and about what we decide to do as a result of what we value.

According to Jesus, to love God is to place God above all else in life. God must be first in all things for us. We are to affirm God, to be with God in prayer, and to serve God in obedience. That emphasis is sounded again and again throughout the scriptures. The first commandment requires it: "Thou shall have no other gods before me!" Jesus made it the primary focus of His teaching. He talked more about the Kingdom of God than about anything else. Of course, in any kingdom, the king comes first. So, in the Kingdom of God, God and God's will takes precedence above all else.

Repeatedly, in sermons and in classes, I have said that the whole world is designed to function in a God centered way. God is to be at the center, with everything else in life deriving its meaning and direction from that vital center. That's the central theme of my book of systematic theology, "The Right Order of Things." The right order of things is life organized with God at the center. Can I say it any more clearly than that? God first. God at the center. And our most earnest prayer being, "Not my will, but Your will be done." That is what it means to love God with all our being. That's the main thing.

All good Jews in both the ancient and modern world would agree with that. It is foundational for them when they are at their best. As much as Jesus also affirmed that, He did not stop with that. More than any other person then or now, Jesus insisted upon linking our love for God with our love for others. What made sense to Jesus is that if you really love God, you will also love all those whom God loves, and that is everyone! After affirming our love for God as the first and great commandment, Jesus added, in a quote from the nineteenth chapter of Leviticus, "A second (commandment) is like it: 'You shall love your neighbor as yourself.'" That completes it, doesn't it? When we have experienced God's love for us and have received that love by faith, the evidence of that is that we love God, we love ourselves, and we love others.

And that is what got Jesus into trouble, that part about loving others. For some reason, throughout history, people of faith have thought that we can pick and choose those we will love. We will love those we like, those we feel good about, those who look like us and think like us, and ignore the others. We will love the worthies and reject the unworthies. Where did we get that idea? Certainly not from Jesus. Jesus said, "So, you love those who love you, do you? You love those who are easy to love, do you? So what! That's easy. Everyone does that, even pagans do that. What are you doing more than others?" Jesus loved everyone: rich and poor, old and young, male and female, well and sick, gay and straight, Jews, Romans, Samaritans, Gentiles. He loved thieves, prostitutes, tax collectors, lepers. Jesus loved everyone! Of course he didn't like everyone. He didn't approve of the behavior of everyone. But Jesus loved everyone, and that got him into trouble. The first century righteous people spat out their condemnation, saying, "This man welcomes sinners, and eats with them!" In the Middle East, if you sit down and share a meal with someone, you are pledging life-long friendship with that someone, and that offended the self-righteous religious leaders of Jesus' day. And they were right, He did love and welcome sinners. He did. As someone has said, "Jesus never lost his taste for bad company." I am glad about that because I am one of them!

What did Jesus mean when He talked about loving? As I have said, loving goes well beyond feeling good about a person or approving of their behavior. To love as Jesus loved is to value a person as a child of God and to treat him or her accordingly. Listen now, I'm about to say something important. The value of a person has nothing whatsoever to do with his or her appearance or behavior. Every person is of infinite worth simply because every person is a child of God and they are to be valued for that reason and for that reason alone. So, we are to value others, to want what is best for them, and in every way within our power to do what is best for them. It's not about feelings. Mature, Christian loving is an act of the will. We decide to love others and to act lovingly toward them because they are children of God and because God loves them. And, a remarkable fact is that the more we act lovingly toward others, the better chance we have to feel loving about them! I remember something Anton Lang once said, as he played the part of Jesus in the Oberammergau Passion Play. He said, "You have no idea how much I have come to love these men as I have washed their feet night after night." Do you hear it? Not, I love them, therefore I wash their feet. No, I wash their feet and as a result I begin to feel love for them.

The most challenging ethical principle I know is found in the words of Jesus in the twenty-fifth chapter of Matthew. Jesus was talking about those to be welcomed into the Kingdom of God. He said, "I was hungry and you gave me food, I was thirsty and you gave me something to drink, I was a stranger and you welcomed me, I was naked and you gave me clothing, I was sick and you took care of me, I was in prison and you visited me." And the people listening to Jesus asked, "When? When did we do all those things for you?" Jesus replied, "Just as you did it to one of the least of these who are members of my family, you did it to me." Later He said, "Just as you did not do it to one of the least of these, you did not do it to me."

Who is it that we put into steel cages, separated from their families, denied adequate nutrition, hygiene, and health care? Who is it? It's Jesus. We don't have to determine who it is we are dealing with, whether worthy or unworthy, legal or illegal, greatest or least. Because it's always Jesus. Always. And if you don't like what I am saying, your argument is not with me, but with Jesus, because that is what He said, "Just as you did it to one of the least of these who are members of my family, you did it to me."

Jesus gave us examples of how to love. At the last supper He washed the disciples' feet and gave us an example of servant love. The next day He went to the cross and gave us an example of suffering love. From the cross He looked out at those who had rejected him, denied him, abandoned him, and crucified him. He looked out at them and loved them. He even prayed for them. And if we are to keep company with Jesus, we are to love as He loved. We are to love everyone, valuing them, wanting what is best for them, and in whatever ways we can, doing what is best for them, even at great cost to ourselves.

I have said that these words of Jesus about loving God, loving ourselves, and loving others point us to the main thing in life. Now, what are we to do with all of that? If we think Christianity is only about doing certain "religious" things out there on the periphery of life, if we think it is enough to come to worship, read the scriptures, think about it, talk about it, pray about it, and then go home and eat fried chicken without the scriptures making a profound difference in the way we live our lives – if we think that, then we have not just missed the main thing, we have missed the whole thing. We have joined that company of people who want God to save us without bothering us!

In the scripture Jesus quoted from Deuteronomy, after we are told to love God with all our being, listen to what it says: "Keep these words that I am commanding you today in your heart. Recite them to your children and talk about them when you are at home and when you are away, when you lie down and when you rise. Bind them as a sign on your hand, fix them as a frontlet on your forehead, and write them on the doorposts of your house and on your gates." Wow! The writer of Deuteronomy is serious!

This scripture is why faithful Jews affix a mezuzah to the entrance of their house or apartment and touch it every time they enter or leave. The mezuzah contains a printed copy of the "Shema," the commandment to love God with all our being. This scripture is also why Orthodox Jews, when they pray, put phylacteries on their arms and foreheads. It's as if this scripture is commanding the faithful to keep this as close to you as you possibly can, to remember it every moment of every day, and to make it a part of you, because this is the main thing in life!

Listen to this continuing emphasis in scripture. When Ezekiel and John of Revelation were called by God to speak to the people, they were instructed to swallow the scrolls given to them by God before they spoke. Swallow the scrolls – what a strange command! Clearly, God is saying that before they spoke to the people, God's word had to become a part of them. Swallow the scroll! Not just God "out there," but God "in here," speaking His word through those in whom

God lives. And Jesus, when He gave us the Sacrament of the Lord's Supper, said, "This is my body. Eat it. This is my blood. Drink it." In other words, Christ is not only present "out there." He must also be invited "in here." He must become a part of us, shaping us, guiding us, empowering us, so that, increasingly, as we live our lives, we reflect his presence and we begin to look and sound like Jesus.

Let me say it again. Scripture is not to be read and discussed and then forgotten. Christianity is not something "tacked on," a pleasant additive, an optional extra, but not making much of a difference in us. No! When Christianity is real for us, it is who we are. It defines us. Not a God out there, but in here. Because God first loved us, with a rich, gracious, never failing love, we are to love God with all our being, we are to love ourselves, and we are to love others, all others, because that's the main thing in life!

One final story. Peter Storey is a Christian pastor in South Africa. During the struggle over apartheid, he was an outspoken advocate for racial justice, racial inclusiveness. That was not a popular stance there in those days, so powerful people saw to it that he was deposed from his pulpit and removed from leadership in the church. But Peter Storey never wavered in his faith and he never compromised his convictions. His faith wouldn't let him. As the years passed, the grace of Christ melted hard hearts, apartheid was abolished, and Storey returned to his pulpit and was restored to leadership, now not only in South Africa, but in the larger world.

On one occasion he was invited to preach in this country. As part of his sermon, he said, "In the United States you have an expression I never heard in South Africa. You talk about 'inviting Jesus into your heart.' I had never heard that before, but I like it, so I decided to do it. I invited Jesus into my heart, and I thought I heard Him say, 'Certainly Peter, I will be happy to come into your heart. But, of course, I will have to bring all my friends with me, and if there is not room in your heart for all my friends, then there is not room in your heart for me either.'"

It is a package deal you know. You can't have God without loving all those whom God loves, because God is love. Invite Jesus into your heart – we used to sing about that at camp. Do you remember?

> "Into my heart, into my heart,
> come into my heart, Lord Jesus.
> Come in today, come in to stay.
> Come into my heart, Lord Jesus."

Of course, today I have to add, "And bring your friends with you. Okay!"

Because God first loved us, we are to love God, to love ourselves, and to love others. Don't ever forget that, because that's the main thing in life!

Prayer: God our Father, teach us about loving. Help us to experience the full extent of Your love for us. Then help us to love You, ourselves, and others, as Jesus did, in whose name we pray. Amen

.

Learning to Love Ourselves

Matthew 22:35-40

She was a beautiful Scandinavian girl. She had come to the hotel room of Dr. and Mrs. Walter Trobisch for counseling, just one day after they had given a lecture at one of the universities of northern Europe. As they discussed her problems, they seemed to come time and again to one basic issue which seemed to be the root of all the others; she could not love herself. In fact, she hated herself so much that she was only a step away from putting an end to her life.

She had been raised in a very religious home. No doubt her parents had been sincere, but they gave her a very distorted understanding of the Christian life. She was afraid to affirm any good thing about herself. She feared that self-appreciation would lead to pride, and pride would mean alienation from God. So, for her, religious faith meant self-deprecation. She believed that self-rejection was the only way to God.

So it was that her religious convictions led her to the brink of suicide. Dr. Trobish took her to a mirror where he asked that she look carefully at her image. She turned away. He held her head gently but firmly, so that she had to look into her own eyes. Obviously the experience caused her emotional pain. Dr. Trobisch asked her to repeat after him:

"I am a beautiful girl... I am a beautiful girl." But that was the one thing she could not do, for in her eyes it was sinful.

I.

I wonder where we ever got the idea that to affirm ourselves... to appreciate ourselves is wrong. Certainly not from Jesus. Because it is quite clear from a careful reading of the gospels that Jesus went around day after day looking for the good in people, pointing it out to them, and asking them to celebrate it. And, in the scripture from the 22nd chapter of Matthew, Jesus tells us to love our neighbors. How? As we love ourselves! Jesus is saying in unmistakable language that we are to love ourselves. Notice that Jesus does not say that we are to love our neighbor instead of ourselves. In fact, in the New Testament the command to love our neighbor is seldom given without an accompanying command to love ourselves. The two are inseparable. So, won't you hear it; Jesus wants us to love ourselves!

Building on those words of Jesus, I want to make a categorical statement which I hope you will remember: It is impossible for you to love yourself too much! To be sure, we can love ourselves in unhealthy, life-negating ways, but that is a problem of kind, not degree. So, I repeat, it is impossible for you to love yourself too much.

What kind of self-love is unhealthy? Well, actually I prefer not to use the term, "self-love" in a negative sense at all. Authentic self-love is always healthy and life-giving. So, let's use the term, "self-centeredness." That's the danger. Self-centeredness is claiming a place for ourselves which belongs only to God. It is centering our life around the reality of self to the exclusion of God and to the exclusion of others. It is pretending to be totally self-sufficient. It is building our lives on the foundation of self. It is deriving all meaning in life from the self. It is looking out and seeing nothing but the self.

What I am talking about is seen in the Greek myth about Narcissus. Narcissus was a youth who was gazing at his reflection in a well one day. The more he stared, the more enamored of himself he became. He fell in love with himself, forgot about everyone and everything else, and totally engrossed with his own image, he tumbled into the water and drowned.

In my judgment, that is not self-love, certainly not in the positive sense of the word. It is self-centeredness, and that is always destructive.

We could all do with less self-centeredness. Life will never work out on that basis. The world was created with God at the center and nothing is good unless we live as if that is so. But let us get it straight once and for all that we don't need less self-love. We can never have too much love for ourselves any more than we can have too much love for God or too much love for our neighbors. They all go together. And there can never be too much love.

In fact, I would go so far as to say that our biggest problem is that we fail to love ourselves enough. Life is diminished in size and demeaned in quality because in large measure our self-esteem is low and our self-appreciation is inhibited. Listen, you can write this down in your book and remember it: however many problems are caused by conceit, a far, far greater number of problems are caused by a low self-image!

I know so many people who sell themselves too short. They will not attempt anything of significance because they have never been able to believe in themselves. Perhaps when they were children they were told that they were dumb, or slow, or ugly, or bad. You supply the adjective, but somewhere along the way someone gave them a negative self-image and they never moved beyond it.

Talk to any counselor, any knowledgeable law enforcement officer and he will confirm in his own experience the words of the scripture: "As a person thinks in his heart, so shall he be." Most criminals have a low self-image, so why try to live up to anything better? Many children born outside of marriage are the direct result of people who do not think highly of themselves. A great many failures in business can be attributed to people who have never come to believe in themselves. And so much of our everyday human discontent is the result of the fact that we are generally much more aware of our weaknesses than our strengths, of our failures than our successes, of our limitations than our gifts. I can't tell you how many problems that creates.

The world is full of people with low self-images who get up in the morning and go off to work feeling that they must somehow prove their worth. They feel that by what they say and do, by what they appear to be, they must earn the approval and acceptance of others. That is a hellish way to live! I can't think of anything worse than to feel that we must prove, earn, achieve, in order to be a worthwhile person. Because, down deep, most of us believe that we can't do it, that we will never be able to measure up!

Do you remember the beautiful Scandinavian girl I mentioned earlier? She confessed that she could not get along with anyone. She was full of criticism and hostility. She thought that her problem was that she loved herself too much. She thought that her self-love kept her from loving others. Actually, just the opposite was true. She could not love others because she had never learned to love herself.

38

Let's not make the same mistake! It is probably true of us as it was true of her — our basic problem is not that we love ourselves too much, but that we love ourselves too little!

II.

So, beginning now, let us stop putting ourselves down. Let us reach out and take hold of some important news about ourselves. Listen carefully: no matter who you are, no matter what your background or experience, there is something about you worth loving because you are a son or daughter of God!

You are a unique person, one of a kind. When God made you, He threw away the mold. God built into you certain gifts and capabilities unlike those of any other human being on earth. Isn't it time we stopped demeaning ourselves and started appreciating the unique gifts God has built into each of us? I don't want to hear anyone say again, "I'm not important... my life doesn't count for much... I can't make any contribution... I don't have any talent."

Can't you see how insulting that is to God? To say that you are without gifts is to discredit God's creation. I can't believe that God would create anyone without a capacity for contribution. I like the idea expressed in tenement district graffiti. There on the alley fence, written with pride in big black letters were the words, "God don't make no junk!" Indeed He doesn't!

Don't worry about thinking too highly of yourself. As long as you remember that all good gifts come from God, to celebrate the good things about you will be an occasion of gratitude rather than of pride. Besides, most of us have a long way to go to catch up with the lofty opinion of mankind revealed in the Bible. The Psalmist wrote: "When I look at

39

your heavens, the work of your fingers, the moon and the stars that you have established; what are human beings that you are mindful of them, mortals that you care for them? For you have made them a little lower than God and crowned them with glory and honor. (Psalm 8:3-5,)"

That is what the Bible thinks of us... "a little lower than God." We are the children of a Father who loves us very much. We are the sons and daughters of God. No, our problem is not in thinking too highly of ourselves. Our problem is in catching up with the Bible's vision of our greatness!

So, if you are good looking, acknowledge that. If you are smart, give thanks for that. If you have an out-going personality, celebrate that. If you have talent, use that. Every gift is from God, so whatever your gifts are, discover them, celebrate them, use them. That's not arrogance, it is honesty. Dizzy Dean used to say, "It's not braggin' if you done it!" Make no mistake about it, you have qualities to affirm, if you will take the time to discover them. What I am suggesting is that you get in touch with the gifts that are yours. Discover all those qualities and experiences that combine to make you who you are. Keep working at all of that until you are able to say, "Hey, it's good to be me!"

But even if our gifts are deeply buried and hard to find, or if they are fewer in number and not quite as impressive as our friends, or if we have misused our gifts and failed to develop them, we can still affirm ourselves as persons of worth.

Open your ears now, because I am going to give you some good news. You can love and affirm yourself, no matter what, because your worth is not dependent upon your ability or your performance. You are a person of worth because you are a child of God... you are one for whom Christ died. If you understand that, then you can love yourself for that best of all possible reasons. Say it to yourself over and over again, "I am a child of God! I am one for whom Christ died!" If God can love me that much, then there must be something in me worth loving!

For the Christian, that is where everything starts. We experience God's love for us. Because of that love, we begin to be able to love ourselves, to appreciate ourselves, to affirm ourselves. Then, loving ourselves, we are able to love our neighbors. That is the way it works. It begins with God, flows through us and extends to our neighbors.

As any good psychologist will tell you, we cannot love our neighbors until we love ourselves. When we do not love ourselves, our attention turns inward, searching for ourselves, trying to understand ourselves. We become obsessed with ourselves. And we spend our lives frantically trying to earn love, achieve respect, prove our worth. Don't you see, it is only when we have received God's love and have come to love ourselves, that we are able to turn our attention to our neighbors and to love them in a gracious, giving way. It is simply a way of passing on to others that which we have received.

III.

I have been talking about the importance of loving ourselves. Now I want to talk about some of the ways in which we do that. Let me suggest several things briefly. First, we accept ourselves as we are, saying "Yes" to the realities of our lives. We agree to be who we are. We stop putting ourselves down for not being like someone else, for not being better looking, for not having more or different talents, for not being in a different situation. We accept ourselves and celebrate "the goodness of being me!" Remember, that is not egoism. It is celebrating the goodness of God's creation. He made you and you're good!

That means accepting limitations as well as strengths. It means refusing to waste time saying, "If only this... wouldn't it be nice if that..." Instead we become like the man who lost a leg in the war. For a while he was bitter and hopeless, spending his days saying, "If only this had not happened." But suddenly something happened to turn everything around and the change in him was dramatic. A friend asked him what happened, and he replied, "I decided to be a one-legged man." Loving yourself means accepting yourself, with both the strengths and weaknesses, the advantages and the limitations that are yours.

Second, to love yourself in a life-giving way means being able to forgive yourself. God has forgiven you, but so many people have difficulty forgiving themselves. Every person is going to make mistakes. All have sinned. There is no one who is perfect. I heard recently about a preacher who asked his congregation if any of them was perfect. No one said anything. Then he asked if they knew anyone who was perfect. A little man in the back raised his hand. "I've never met him, but I've heard a lot about him. He was my wife's first husband."

All humor aside, none of us is perfect. We have all done things we aren't proud of. The guilt of that tends to weight us down and hold us back. But God doesn't intend for us to live with guilt. That is what sunsets are for – to ring down the curtain on a day. God wants to cut us free from everything we failed in today, to help us learn from all that, and then to try it again His way tomorrow. Whatever your past has been, it doesn't have to cast a shadow on your future. God has forgiven you, learn to forgive yourself.

A final aspect of loving yourself is to remember constantly who you are. You are somebody. You are a person of worth. You are a son or daughter of God. That self-mage will help shape our lives in profound ways. If we really see ourselves as God's children, then certain kinds of behavior become unthinkable. If we are God's children, then a certain style of living is expected. It is true, "As a person thinks in his heart, so shall he be."

The other side of that coin is important to note. We can begin to love ourselves and affirm ourselves for no other reason than that we are God's children, loved and affirmed by Him. But in order to continue loving ourselves over a long period of time, we must be able to like ourselves. And that means becoming likable persons. It means becoming worthy of our own self-respect.

I remember a poem by Edgar Guest which Patricia's parents gave to her and which my parents gave to me during our early years. The words are good companions to grow with:

> I have to live with myself, and so
> I want to be fit for myself to know;
> I want to be able as days go by
> Always to look myself straight in the eye;
> I don't want to stand with the setting sun
> And hate myself for the things I've done.
>
> I don't want to keep on a closet shelf
> A lot of secrets about myself,
> And fool myself as I come and go
> Into thinking that nobody else will know
> The kind of person I really am;
> I don't want to dress myself up in sham.

I want to go out with my head erect,
I want to deserve all men's respect;
And here in the struggle for fame and pelf,
I want to be able to like myself.
I don't want to think as I come and go
That I'm bluster and bluff and empty show.

I never can hide myself from me,
I see what others may never see,
I know what others may never know,
I never can fool myself – and so,
Whatever happens I want to be
Self-respecting and conscience free."

You can never get away from you. You are stuck with yourself. So you had better become a person you can like. And it is o.k. to like yourself. It is good to love yourself. In fact, it is a necessity.

According to the New Testament, there are three steps to the good life: Love God – as a result of that you can love yourself – as a result of that, you can love your neighbor.

Prayer: Loving God, our Father, save us from thinking less highly of ourselves than we ought to think. Forgive us for thinking that denying ourselves and putting ourselves down is what You want us to do. Remind us again that You love us and are for us. Impress upon us that each of us is unique, special, and of infinite worth. Never let us forget that the one, over-riding, all-important fact about our lives is that we are Your sons and daughters. We are those for whom Christ has died. Enable us to celebrate that and to give thanks for that. Help us to love ourselves in the same gracious, life-giving way that You love us. In the Master's name we pray. Amen.

Which Side Is Up?

Luke 10:38-42

One afternoon, a Japanese freighter was being unloaded in Los Angeles harbor. Gigantic cranes were lifting crates of merchandise from the hold of the ship and placing them on the docks below. The intriguing thing was that each container had unusual handling instructions printed on the side in bold black letters. The writing was both in English and Japanese. Normally you would expect an arrow with the word "Up" printed beside it. Such simple, concise language is usually sufficient. But such was not the case with these containers. On each of them these words were printed: "If this side is up, this carton is upside down!"

I find sermons everywhere, and when I heard that story I knew that there was a sermon in it, so here it is! I believe that there are at least two sides — two dimensions to life. There is the functional side and there is the relational side. The functional dimension has to do with the jobs we do, the tasks we undertake, the projects we attempt. The relational dimension has to do with what is happening between people while we are functioning.

Now, both dimensions are essential. We cannot live without either of them. But in every life one will be more important than the other. The question is, which side is up?

Which side is most important to you? I believe that your honest answer to that question will determine in large measure how happy and how fulfilled you are in life. If the wrong side is up, your life will be upside down!

I.

Jesus understood that both dimensions are important. Certainly there are functions we are to perform. We all have jobs to do. I admire those people who accept a task, take it seriously, analyze what is required for its successful completion, and give their best efforts toward it. Thank God for people like that. We all depend upon them. The world would be chaotic without them You will find no support from Jesus for laziness, sloppiness, or ineffectiveness. No, the carpenter from Nazareth knew the value of hard work, quality work. Dedicated, effective functioning is important, make no mistake about it.

But, as important as it is to function well, Jesus insisted upon the primary importance of relationships. In fact, I cannot for the life of me think of a better single word to describe the meaning of life than that word, "relationship." If I understand life at all, I understand that our primary purpose is to be in a loving, trusting relationship with God and that, as a result, we are able to enjoy close, caring, helping relationships with others. Both the functional and the relational dimensions of life are essential, but unless the relational side is up and primary in your life, your life is upside down.

The story I read for scripture says it. Jesus went for a visit to the home of Mary and Martha. Martha was a conscientious homemaker. She was busy cleaning the house, preparing the food, meeting the needs of all in the household. She was as busy as a beaver scurrying around with all of her functioning. But all the while, Mary just sat with Jesus, listening to Him, talking with Him, enjoying being with Him. Martha became angry that she was having to do all of the work. She asked Jesus to "tell her to help me." Jesus replied that Mary had made the better choice, that what she was doing was more important than what Martha was doing.

Of course we have to eat, and someone has to do the work. So Jesus would never deny the essential importance of what Martha was doing. The danger as Jesus saw it was that Martha would spend all of her time with busy work, performing a thousand and one tasks, until He had to leave and as a result they would not have been together. That is always the danger, isn't it? We busy ourselves with so many important tasks... we spend all of our time and energy functioning and never get around to relating. Mary said, in effect, the busy work can wait. I don't want to miss being with Jesus. And Jesus said that Mary's priorities were right side up!

That's a word we would do well to hear. Our children are with us for a short while, then they grow up and leave home. We develop friendships and then we are separated by a move. Our loved ones die. Change is constant, and all too often we are forced to say "goodbye" to those close to us. We wonder where the time went. We find it difficult to understand why we spent so little time enjoying one another, and why the words, "I love you," were so seldom upon our lips. Sadly, many of us discover too late that relationships are far more important than we knew.

Again and again in the gospels Jesus showed us that relationships are primary. Do you remember the time that some little children were brought to Him for His blessing? The disciples thought that Jesus didn't have the time for children. After all, He had work to do, miracles to perform,

47

multitudes to teach. They wanted to get on with the job. But Jesus always had time for people. He had the idea that relationships with people are central to the meaning of life. So He rebuked the disciples and said, "Let the children come to Me. Do not hinder them. For to such belongs the Kingdom of God." (Matthew 19:14) He picked the children up, placed them in his lap, and loved them. With all the tasks before him, none was more important than that. Relationship!

II.

It is clear that the relational side of life was primary for Jesus. The question is, which side is up for us? Do we relate to people in order to facilitate our functioning? Or do we function in order to make relationship possible? For example, if I am a salesman, am I nice to people in order to get their names on the dotted line? Or, do I see my sales position as a means of relating to people, and the money I make helping to pay the freight so that I can enjoy being with my family and friends? That's an important question. Which, really, is more important for you functioning or relating?

Martin Buber, the eminent Jewish theologian, was getting at the same question when he wrote about the two basic kinds of relationships. The first is the "I-It" relationship, in which we do not treat persons as persons, but as things to be used. We manipulate people to accomplish our desired ends. We use them to reach our goals. The second relationship Buber wrote about was the "I-Thou" relationship in which we treat others as valued human beings to be loved and cared about.

I am very much afraid that most human relationships fall into the "I-It" category. We have learned very well how to get things done. We move people around and manipulate them to accomplish our purposes, but we don't get to know them as persons and we don't touch beneath the surface level. So much of our relating is on the level of: "How are you today?" "Fine, thank you, how are you?" "Fine, thank you." We go through the motions of that without really seeing one another and without really touching one another. Someone has likened us human beings to a bag of marbles – close together spacially, but touching one another only at the outside edges. And that is sad, because when we do that we're missing life. We're missing the joy of being human.

We pass by people every day without seeing them. We work with people, we function with them without ever getting to know them... really know them. I mean knowing who they love, where they hurt, what they care about, what they long for. If we never get beneath the surface to those deeper places... if we do not deal with one another with sensitivity and caring, then we have ceased to be authentically human. If all we do is function together, then no matter how impressive our functioning, we are little more than robots or machines. We've stopped being human, because humanness involves sensitivity, caring, relating!

I am afraid this sort of thing happens at home as well as at work among our friends. Just think about how much of our time and energy at home is spent getting things done. The shopping, cooking, cleaning, sewing, repairing, improving, building, bill-paying, car-pooling, problem-solving, TV watching. I could go on and on. But I wonder what would happen in our homes if suddenly all our tasks were taken from us and we had to spend all our time relating, what would we do? For all too many families it would be a totally unique experience! So much of what we call "being together' involves being together spacially or functionally, but not emotionally. Even in families, we often do not touch except at the outer edges. We keep even our loved ones at arms length. Oh, we may spend time together. We may get things done in cooperation with one another. But we do not touch in our depths, and even when we are in the presence of one another we feel alone. A saddened wife said recently about her husband: "He is always a thousand miles away. He will not let anyone close to him beyond the level of friendly exchange: me, the children, his parents – even God."

When I talk about relationship, I am talking about being with someone and not just alongside him. I'm talking about the experience of risking openness with someone, the experience of touching beneath the surface. It's the experience of looking into one another's eyes, really looking, and knowing that at least for that moment you are the whole world for one another. It's the experience of listening to one another and knowing that not only your words but also your feelings are being heard. It's the experience of knowing that whatever is the deepest truth about your life, you can share it and know that it is o.k., that you will be loved and cared about anyway.

Relationship is the experience of being with a caring person who will not judge or condemn or pretend to be superior in any way. Nor will they rush in to give advice before it is asked for. It's being with someone who understands that the first question in any authentic communication is not, "Do you agree?" or "Do you approve?" No, the first question is, "Do you understand and do you care?" Relationship is the experience of two people being "with" one another, caring about one another, and saying to one another, "I hear, I understand, I care, I am with you."

Such an experience is an experience of incredible intimacy. It is the most life-giving experience in all the world. It is what life is all about. And it is far too important to be so rare!

I look around me and I see a world full of lonely people. We long for relationship, but at the same time we are afraid of it. We busy ourselves with all kinds of tasks, we surround ourselves with large numbers of people, hoping that our loneliness can be overcome and our needs met. But usually we are disappointed because we keep people at arms length. We are afraid of relationship.

George Bernard Shaw once remarked that he could never admire a lion tamer's courage, because when the tamer was in the cage with the lions at least people could not get to him.

We are frightened of people. We are afraid if we let down our defenses and let people see us as we are, they may not like us or love us. We are afraid if we let people get too close to us, they will take advantage of us or make too many demands upon us. So we play it safe and keep them away, and in the process we rob ourselves of life.

We try to impress people. We try to make people approve of us. And the way we do that is by putting our best foot forward. We want to do our jobs better than anyone else. We want to be right. We want to be good. We want to be strong. If we can do all of that... or at least if we can make others think that we have done all of that, then maybe they will love us. So our thinking goes. But that line of thinking is upside down!

Listen! Let me tell you something important. (And I hope you will hear me loud and clear!) If you appear always to be competent, right, strong, and good, other people will admire you and respect you. But they will not love you, they will not identify with you, and they will not get close to you. People will love you and get close to you only when you let them know that you are human as they are... human with

51

feelings, longings, hurts, disappointments, weaknesses, and all of those other things that all of us human beings have. Admiration and respect are fine, but there comes a time when we will trade all of that for a little love, a little closeness, a sense of belonging to someone.

I hope we can learn once and for all that we touch one another not at that point of strength, but at that point of weakness in our lives. Intimacy comes only when we allow someone else to see our vulnerability. If you are not willing to risk that you will never know closeness. And you will never know love. My friend Maxie Dunnam said it in his book, "Dancing at my Funeral." He said, "Living depends on loving. Loving depends on knowing. And knowing depends on risking." He's right.

Not too long ago, a father shared a special experience with me. He had done a number of things he was not proud of. He had failed himself, his wife, and his children. He had always been a proud, strong man. It was not easy to admit his failure. But he sensed that somehow he had to confess to his children and ask their forgiveness. Somehow he had to make it right. He had never had to do anything so difficult. He had always wanted his children to think of him as strong and good. But he mustered all his courage, went into their room, told them he had failed, and that he wanted their forgiveness, and that together they could start over again. And do you know what happened? The very thing he feared was the means by which a new life was begun. He said, "Jim, I've never been as close to my children as I was that night." Of course! They could identify with his frail humanness. They felt needed in his weakness. Perhaps for the first time in their lives, they knew that they had something they could give to their father. Finally, here was a person they could get close to!

We may be admired for our strength and rightness, but we are loved and deeply touched only at the point of our weakness. I'm sure of that!

Well, those are the two sides of life; the functional and the relational. Both are important, but the relational is primary. It doesn't matter how much you accomplish functionally... you may perform and achieve in ways that stagger the imagination... but if you have not made meaningful contact with people, if you are not loving and being loved by people, then you have missed it. The wrong side is up. And you are in danger of functioning and dying without having lived.

Martha, we commend you for your conscientiousness. We applaud the seriousness with which you approach your task. But don't overlook people. People don't exist for the food you are so intent upon serving. The food exists for the people. So, function well, yes; but also, as a matter of first priority, make time for relationships!

There is a story which illustrates what I mean by the word, "Relationship." I share it in closing. Perhaps you remember the name Sam Rayburn. He was one of the most powerful men in Washington during his tenure as Speaker of the House. He liked to say that he had not served under eight president, but with eight presidents. He enjoyed instant access to the White House by a side door. His power and influence were immense!

But there was a side to the man which you may not know. One day he heard that the teenage daughter of a Capitol Hill reporter had died. Early the following morning there was a knock on the reporter's door, and when he opened it he found Speaker Rayburn standing there, "I just came by," he said.

The grieving father invited him in, and Rayburn sat with the family. Finally he asked, "Have you had your morning coffee?" The reporter said they had not taken time, so the Speaker quickly said that he could at least make coffee for them.

While he was working in the kitchen, the reporter came and said, "Mr. Speaker, I just remembered that you were supposed to be having breakfast at the White House this morning. "Well, I was," said Rayburn, "but I called the President and told him I had a friend I wanted to be with."

I am sure that the Speaker of the United States House of Representatives had a great many important tasks to perform that day, many tasks indeed! But he made time for relationship! Relationship! If that side is not up, then your life is upside down!

Prayer: God our Father, most of us do not so many bad things. But we busy ourselves and distract ourselves with so many second class good things that the best is crowded out. With all of the important things we have to do, help us to see people. Help us to be open to people. Help us to care about people. Father, give us life by giving us deep meaningful relationships. Put our lives right side up by teaching how to love and how to be loved. In Jesus' name we pray. Amen.

A Burden or a Song?

Is your religion a load or a lift? That was a popular sermon topic during my growing up years. Preachers were fascinated with alliterations – load/lift – and they thought the idea was a catchy one, so I heard more sermons on the subject than I wanted to hear. Frankly, I never cared much for them. Do you know of ideas like that, ideas that turn you off sometimes? I thought it was a pointless question. I thought the preachers were just setting up straw men only to knock them down again. After all, the answer to the question should be obvious to all Christians. Of course our religion is supposed to be a lift rather than a load. It's supposed to be a help rather than a hindrance. Why even raise the question? The answer should be obvious!

There is a song in the old Cokesbury Hymnal which we used to sing. The words, still fresh in my memory, proved my point:

> "Jesus took my burden I could no longer bear,
> Yes, Jesus took my burden in answer to my prayer;
> My anxious fears subsided, my spirit was made strong,
> For Jesus took my burden and left me with a song."

55

I would sing that song and think to myself, "Now that's the way it's supposed to be." Any religion able to trade a burden for a song has got to be okay, right? Any religion able to do that has got to give a lift to your spirit! That's the way it's supposed to be. That's what looks and sounds like Jesus to me. Any authentic Christianity ought to remove our burdens, or at least make them more manageable. And that will make us feel like singing – thus, a burden exchanged for a song. That's the way it's supposed to be. But, as I have gained more experience in life, I've learned that hard lesson that there is often a difference between what is supposed to be and what is.

That's the first thing I want to say. The fact is, a great many people do not experience religion as a lift. Instead, it is an additional load for them to bear. If they were honest they would say, "Jesus took my song and left me with a burden!" That's not the way it is supposed to be, but for too many people, that's the way it is.

Religion, for them, involves rules, regulations, obligations, and responsibilities. Instead of removing weight from our daily load, it adds to it. God is not experienced as a loving Father who wants only the best for his children. Instead, God is experienced as a stern taskmaster. God is seen as a patrolman in the sky, wanting to cut down on our speed and make us obey all the rules.

I hope I'm wrong, but I fear that the prevalent image of the Christian gospel goes something like this: God wants us all to be good. And God has given us the Bible to show us how to be good. God watches our every move and records our behavior in a grade book. We receive a gold star for every good deed we do, and a black mark for every bad deed. When we die, God adds up the gold stars and black marks. If we have more gold stars than black marks we go to heaven. If we

56

have more black marks than gold stars we go to hell. And that's the Christian gospel! That's the gospel? The word, "gospel" means "good news," and I ask you, where is the good news in that? That's not good news, that's bad news! If that is what Christianity is, if that is the way it works, we are all in trouble!

According to that understanding of Christianity, this is a reward and punishment world in which we are rewarded for keeping the rules and punished for breaking them. And my, how many rules there are! We are supposed to go to worship, read the Bible, say our prayers, tithe our incomes, love our enemies, serve our neighbors, give to those in need, go the second mile, turn the other cheek, and on and on it goes. We're supposed to do all of those things, and more, smiling all the time, while refraining from lying, cheating, stealing, swearing, and being unkind to children, pets, and mothers-in-law! I get tired just thinking about it all! It's a heavy weight to carry! And woe be to us if we mess up!

With that picture of the Christian life in mind, I can understand why a great many people want no part of it. I can understand the response one man made. A friend said to him one day, "Wouldn't you like to be a Christian?" He answered, "No thanks, I have enough trouble as it is!"

I am saddened by the number of people who have such a distorted understanding of the Christian life — life seen primarily as rules, regulations, and obligations. There is no joy in such a religion. There is no lifting of the load. Instead, Jesus takes our song and replaces it with a burden. I tell you, if that's what the Christian faith is all about, I want no part of it!

In the first century world of Jesus, most people experienced religion primarily as a religion of rules. There were hundreds and hundreds of rules they were to obey. Jesus came into that legalistic world and began to talk about the primacy of relationships. According to Jesus, the important thing is to have the right kind of relationship with God, with ourselves, and with our neighbors. Jesus said that when we experience God's love for us, and then allow that love to begin shaping our lives, then we receive from God everything we need to do the things that God calls us to do.

Listen now, I'm about to say something important. When the right thing is happening, the emphasis in the Christian faith is not primarily about what God demands; the emphasis is upon what God gives. God gives us love in Jesus. Once we receive that, trust that, and begin to live our lives according to the guidance and strength of that, then we begin to be able to live lives that look and sound like Jesus. Do you understand? God shapes our lives not by passing down a lot of rules from "out there," but by loving and empowering us from "in here."

Jesus insisted that God wants us to have all the best that life affords. Jesus said, "I have come that you may have life, and have it abundantly!" (John 10:10) Do you hear it? The emphasis is not on demands – which add to the load we are carrying. The emphasis is upon gifts – those gifts God gives us to exchange our burden for a song. This is not to say that there are no demands – there are, heavy demands. There is a cost to discipleship, a cost to following Jesus. But, in God's love for us, God always gives us enough grace to meet the demands.

Sad to say, the first century religious leaders did not understand. Even Jesus' disciples did not understand at first. And, a great many professing Christians still don't get it. I sometimes think that it may be better to have no religious faith at all than to be caught up in the distorted, legalistic religion I have been describing. You've heard it said, "A little learning is a dangerous thing." That's true, but a little religion is even more dangerous than that. A small dose of distorted religious faith seems to diminish life rather than to enlarge it. It is life negating rather than life enhancing. It's the worst of all worlds. Someone described such a person as "too Christian to enjoy their sinning, and too sinful to enjoy their Christianity." That's the worst place of all to be!

My father told about the time, when he was a boy, and he and his friends were out playing "follow the leader." The leader would jump a stump and all of them would jump the stump. The leader would run around a fence and all of them would run around a fence. Then the leader jumped across a creek. And, just as my father started to jump, someone shouted, "Stop!" My father sort of jumped and sort of didn't. As a result, he landed squarely in the water. It's better to jump or not jump. The worst choice of all is to "sort of" jump. Similarly, to be "sort of" religious is the worst option of all. The narrow, legalistic religion I have described lays on the obligation, but withholds the power. It lays on the duty, but withholds the blessing. That's the worst place of all to be!

Let's look again at the scripture from the fifth chapter of Matthew. When you read Jesus' words about going the second mile, turning the other cheek, returning good for evil, and loving your enemies, how do you feel? And if all of that were not difficult enough, when Jesus concludes by saying, "Be perfect," how does that make you feel?

Does it feel like a huge load to carry? Does it come across to you primarily as an obligation? Do you feel that you have to measure up to all of that in order to be loved by God? Are you afraid of not measuring up to God's expectations?

59

If that's what you feel, then your religion probably *is* more of a burden than a song. But I'm convinced that is not what God wants for us. When I read the Bible as a whole, I begin to believe that what God wants to give us far outweighs what God asks of us. Whatever God asks us to do, God gives us everything we need to do it. I believe that, but most people don't. I fear that most people have just enough religion to make them miserable, but not enough to make them blessed. If we are caught up in a narrow, legalistic world in which the dominant word we hear is "You ought. You should. You must," then that is a heavy load to carry, and life is probably experienced as a gray, joyless, duty-filled burden.

Thank God, that is not the way the Bible, as a whole, looks at life. From the Christian perspective, life is not drudgery, but a celebration. God is a Father who is with us and for us. God's intent is not to place additional weight upon us, but to take weight off. Even when God asks us to do something, it is because the fullest possible life is in that direction. And, God is always willing to give us everything we need to do it. So, God not only asks, God also enables. The Cokesbury song was right after all. God wants to take our burdens and leave us with a song.

It was Alfred North Whitehead who described the religious quest as moving from God the void, to God the enemy, and from God the enemy to God the friend. I think there is wisdom in that description. First, there is nothing – we are not aware of God at all – God the void. Then, when we first become aware of God, God is the enemy. God is the one who lays on us all the rules, the responsibilities, and the obligations. We sense that God is not really for us, in fact, if we don't measure up, God will punish us. At the feeling level, that feels like an enemy no matter how much we talk about God's love. And so many people never get past that stage. Even though they would never say it, and perhaps are never consciously aware of it, God is experienced as the enemy, and religion is a huge weight around their necks, inhibiting joy, and holding them back.

Now, obviously, that is not the way it is supposed to be. But it is only when we grow up, and begin to mature in our faith, that we are able to experience God as friend, One who is not against us, but for us. God doesn't just make demands of us, even more God wants to give to us.

Just listen to the encouraging words of scripture: "I have come that you may have life, and have it abundantly." (John 10:10) "These things I have spoken to you that my joy may be in you, and that your joy may be full. (John 15:11) "My grace is sufficient for you." (2 Corinthians 12:9) "Peace I leave with you, my peace I give to you. But not as the world gives do I give to you. Let not your hearts be troubled, neither let them be afraid." (John 14:27) "I can do all things through Christ who strengthens me." (Philippians 4:13) "They who wait upon the Lord shall renew their strength; they shall mount up with wings as eagles; they shall run and not be weary; they shall walk and not faint." (Isaiah 40:31)

Do you hear it? Do you hear all of those gifts that God wants to give us? As God intends it, life is to be an adventure, a blessing, and a celebration. What God wants is for our faith to enable us to spread our wings and fly! That's the nature of authentic Christianity!

Now let me share with you what makes the difference, the difference between religion as a burden and religion as a joy. Part of it has to do with the seriousness of our commitment. A luke-warm, half-hearted Christianity will never be satisfying. "Sort of" Christianity lays on the obligation but denies the blessing. No, you have to be serious about your faith if you are going to move from God, the enemy, to God, the friend.

But, as important as serious intent is, it is not the most important thing. The most important thing in life is how we understand and experience God. It is essential to know in our depths that God is not against us, but for us, to know that God is like Jesus, loving us with a love beyond our understanding. And, it is essential to make the transition from a God "out there," telling us what to do, to a God "in here" blessing us, helping us to become all that we can be, and helping us to do what God calls us to do. It makes all the difference in the world to understand that we receive God's gifts not because we have obeyed God's rules; no, not that; rather we are more able to obey God's rules because we first have received God's gifts!

Look again at the fifth chapter of Matthew in that light. What if we heard these words of Jesus not so much as demands to be obeyed, but as gifts to be received? What if God is saying to us, not "These are things you must do," but "this is the kind of person I will help you to become"? Doesn't that change everything?

Take that most difficult verse of all, the one about being perfect. What if "be perfect" is not so much a commandment as it is a promise? And what if perfection really means "completion," the complete you, the complete person God has created you to be? What if that is not something God demands, but something God wants to give? Do you see the difference?

When we understand it, the God we have come to know in Jesus is not a God "out there" making demands upon us, but a God "in here" giving us everything we need, and enabling us to grow into the persons God intends us to be! I tell you, that is good news! I can sing about that!

A friend of mine died not too long ago. He had been struggling with heart disease for a long time. Years before his death, he had six arterial by-passes in a long and tedious surgery. When he came home after that near death experience, I went to see him. We talked about all he had gone through, and he wanted to talk about his faith. Tears came into his eyes as he said, "Jim, it's too bad I've had to go through this, but in the midst of it all, I experienced something real. I experienced for myself the truth of the 23rd Psalm: 'Even though I walk through the valley of the shadow of death, I will fear no evil, for thou art with me.'"

As I looked into his eyes, I knew he was talking about a powerful, personal experience. He had been through it. He knew. I didn't have to ask him whether his faith was a burden or a song. His faith was the most real thing in his life! His faith was his single greatest source of meaning and strength and hope. Of course it's a song, a song of joy! And that's the way it's supposed to be.

Let's all grow to experience our faith in that way. Let's not exchange a song for a burden. Let's exchange our burden for a song!

Prayer: Loving Father, save us from the shallows of faith which blind us to your love and distort your purposes for us. Help us to grow up to a mature faith that looks and sounds like Jesus, a faith experienced not as rules, but as gifts, not as a burden, but as a joy. In Jesus' name we pray. Amen.

Christians Without Wax

Matthew 23:27-28

I have always been fascinated by the origin of words. Take the word "sincere," for example. Do you know its beginnings? In ancient times, wealthy people liked to adorn their houses and courtyards with statues. Unscrupulous business people would often take marble statuary that contained either faulty material or poor workmanship and cover up the blemishes with wax. After polishing, only a trained eye could detect the wax, so they could sell the statues for top dollar. But, with the passage of time, the wax would deteriorate and fall out, revealing the sub-standard work of art. The practice was so prevalent that reputable and skilled craftsmen began labeling their work, "sine cera," that is, without wax. That's the origin of our word, "sincere," To be sincere then, is to be a person without wax, without phoniness, without a cosmetic cover up. What you see is what you get!

Again and again in the gospels we find Jesus pleading for that kind of sincerity. He insisted that there should be a harmony between the inner person and the outer expression, a harmony between the motive and the deed. He had little patience with those people who were more concerned with

65

their appearance than with their essence. Although Jesus criticized sinful behavior in all its forms, his sharpest rebukes were reserved for those who pretended to be something they were not, those who tried to cover up their blemishes with wax while pretending that they were without fault.

The scripture in the twenty-third chapter of Matthew contains one such rebuke. Here is the context: according to Jewish law, a dead body was unclean. If you touched it, you would become unclean and would be barred from entering the Temple or synagogue until you had gone through rites of purification. Likewise, to touch a tomb would render you unclean. Often tombs would line roadsides and there was a danger of coming into contact with them inadvertently. Whether intentional or not, if you touched one, you would become unclean. So, to call attention to them, the tombs would be whitewashed. The whitewash was like a sign saying, "Stay away! Unclean!" At the same time, the whitewash did make them stand out in the bright light of day, making them rather attractive.

So, Jesus used that image to describe many of the Scribes and Pharisees whom He called "hypocrites." He said, "On the outside you appear to be righteous, but on the inside you are full of dead men's bones and all uncleanness." He called them "hypocrites." That's another word whose origin we would do well to explore. It's a good word when properly used, but it is thrown around rather loosely and often distorted by some. Let me make an important distinction: a hypocrite is not someone who fails to live up to his or her ideals. That would describe most of the best people I know. I would hate to have ideals so low that I can live up to them. No, a hypocrite is not someone who fails to live up to high ideals. A hypocrite is someone who *pretends* to be something he or she never *intends* to be. Hypocrites are not concerned with *becoming*, they are obsessed with *appearing*.

No doubt Jesus got that Greek word, "hypocrite" from the theater. There was a theater in the town of Sepphoris, a short distance from Jesus' home town of Nazareth. Biblical scholars believe that Joseph and Jesus likely found work in the much larger city of Sepphoris where they worked with stone as well as wood in the building trade. There, Jesus was exposed to urban Roman and Greek culture, including the theater. The word, "hypocrite" is a theatrical term. An actor who pretended to be someone else was a "hypocrite."

Jesus would say to his first century contemporaries and to us, "Get rid of the wax. You don't need it. Stop pretending. Let there be a congruence between who you are and who you appear to be. Be real, and then we'll go from there."

It is so clear to me that as long as we insist upon pretending, we separate ourselves from reality. And when we separate ourselves from reality, all the relationships of life begin to go wrong. How can we have any meaningful relationship with God as long as we continue hiding from God, projecting success images in His direction, pretending to be someone we are not? How can other people relate to us if they never know when they are seeing a real person or some veneer covering over our appearance? And how can we know whether others love us or whether they love that phony person we are pretending to be? Isn't it clear? There can be no real relationship unless there is a touching of soul to soul, of substance to substance, of reality to reality. Relationship requires reality without wax cover up! Sine cera – sincerity!

That is why I am troubled to see how many Christians think they have to pretend. We pick up our wax at the door of the church, and we fill in the cracks and imperfections on the way to our seats. Then we are able to sit with others as highly polished, perfect people! With that understanding, so much of our religious activity becomes a matter of applying cosmetics to our appearance rather than allowing God to redeem the reality.

That troubles me. It troubles me because everything I know about the Christian gospel tells me that we can be ourselves in the presence of God. We don't have to be phony around God because with God's love and forgiveness, whatever is the reality of our lives, we can bring that with us and know that we will still be treated with that love and forgiveness. Whatever our flaws, God will forgive and begin to shape them into something good. And, whatever about our lives is already good, God will enlarge and use to accomplish His good will. So, we don't have to pretend. I am fond of saying that whenever Christians get together, it's God's way of having a "come as you are" party!

Let's look briefly at two ways people of faith are inclined to pretend. First, we are inclined to pretend that we are better than we are. I don't know where we got the idea that Christianity is primarily concerned about our goodness. Probably we have all heard testimonies in which people have said that before their conversion they were bad, and because of God's grace they now are good. Certainly it is true that the life of faith will take us as we are and begin to shape us into more loving and helpful people. If that is not happening, if we are not growing in those ways, something is wrong.

But I become nervous around people who think of themselves as being good. And I am in good company with that because Jesus, too, had problems with it. Someone came to Jesus one day and addressed Him as "Good Master." Jesus stopped him and said, "Don't call me good. There is only one who is good and that is God." (Mark 10:17-18) I am all in favor of goodness, but I am uncomfortable about "goody goodness." You know what I mean. There is no person so difficult to be around as the person who is good and won't let you forget it for a moment! As Disraeli once commented about Gladstone, "He had not one redeeming defect!"

Look at the people the church calls "saints." We call them good, and in many ways certainly they were, but not one of them thought they were. They were concerned with how much they still needed to grow, to become. It's like, once you think of yourself as a saint, you're disqualified. I heard about a man to whom they gave a medal for his humility, but they had to take it away from him because he started to wear it!

Read the gospels. Jesus much preferred the company of those who were sinners and knew it, and wanted help with it, to those who appeared to be righteous and were proud of it. That stuffy, self-righteous, self-congratulatory image makes us all uncomfortable. When we acknowledge the reality of our lives, and confess it, God can work with that. God can move us from where we are to where we are called to be. But how can God deal with us redemptively as long as we are pretending?

One of the few religious bumper stickers I like is the one that says, "Christians are not perfect, we're just forgiven." Of course. We're not perfect and we don't have to pretend that we are. It is clear to me that when we feel that we must pretend, we are denying the reality of God's grace and the power of God's forgiveness. What a difference it would make if we could come to a new understanding of that in the church and help those outside the church to understand it in that new way as well. The church is not a showcase for saints, but a hospital for sinners. The church is the only organization I know that has as a requirement for membership that we acknowledge that we are not worthy to be members. Do you know anyone else in the world who operates like that? So, if you are already as good as you want or need to be, you probably won't fit in very well in the church, because in the church we are all sinners, still in need of God's love and forgiveness.

Do you understand? Among God's people, of all places, we don't have to pretend. We acknowledge going in that we are all sinners. We start there, and by God's amazing grace, we begin to grow and become more than we were. Please understand once and for all, the point is not our goodness, but God's amazing grace and forgiveness. That is what the Christian gospel is all about. And because of that, we don't have to pretend to be better than we are.

A second inclination is the inclination to pretend to know more than we know. Again, I don't know why. Where does it say that Christians are supposed to have an answer for every question? I don't know about you, but the longer I live, not only do I have fewer answers, I keep discovering more difficult questions.

Again, I am uncomfortable in the presence of people who insist upon giving smug, pat answers to the deepest, most perplexing questions of life. In case you haven't noticed, I readily admit that there are a great many questions I cannot answer. I can't tell you exactly what is waiting for us on the other side of death. I don't know when the end of human history will come. I don't know why growth has to be so painful. I can't explain so much of the suffering and evil in the world. I don't know why it is so much easier to destroy than to build. I don't know why in order to love you have to be open to the possibility of hurt. I can't tell you exactly what God's will is in every situation. I can't even tell you why God decided to create mosquitoes!

Now let me give you the biggest confession of all: it doesn't bother me that I can't answer all questions. When I became a parent, I discovered the endless variety of questions that can be asked. For a while I tried to answer every question posed, because after all, daddies are supposed to know everything. Right? I remember a family going out for a Sunday afternoon drive. While enjoying the various sights of nature, the small son began asking questions. "Daddy, how tall is that tree?" "I don't know, son." "Daddy, how deep is that lake?" "I don't know." "Daddy, how high is that mountain?" "I don't know." "Daddy, do you mind me asking all these questions?" His reply was a classic: "Of course not, son. How else can you learn?" After hearing so many questions from our children when they were young, I learned some magic words, and I have been using them frequently ever since. Here are the magic words: "I don't know."

I am convinced that for us Christians to insist upon being able to answer every question is really evidence of our insecurity and lack of faith. Christianity does not promise an answer to every question, but a loving, strengthening relationship with God in every life experience. I don't have all the answers, but God does, and that's good enough for me.

Hear that! Faith does not give us all the answers. Faith allows us to go on living well even when some of our questions go unanswered. Faith does not solve all our problems for us. Faith enables us to keep on going even when our problems remain. Our security is not in information. Our security is in a trusting relationship with God!

If you know me at all, you know I'm going to keep on asking questions. God gave me a mind and I know God wants me to use it. I want to question and understand everything as best I can. But I'm not going to be too

71

uncomfortable if, at the end of the inquiry, there are still questions I cannot answer. And I will not pretend to know more than I know.

I wonder who we are trying to impress with our pretending. Are we trying to impress other people? Well, sooner or later they will see through our façade. And even if they don't, our pretending separates us from them. You can't have a close, genuine relationship with a make-believe person. You just can't. And it is awfully lonely there behind the wax cover up.

And, if we are trying to impress God with our pretending, forget it. You can't deceive God. God sees us just as we are. When we pretend with God, all we can accomplish is deceiving ourselves into thinking we have no need of God, and the only one we have deceived then is ourselves.

When we really understand the Christian gospel, we will know that there is no need to pretend about anything, because salvation is not by our goodness, or by our wisdom, or by our strength, or by our accomplishments, or by anything else that we do. Salvation is by God's grace and God's grace alone. It is an unconditional gift!

That's why we can be who we are. We can acknowledge the sin for which we need forgiveness. We can acknowledge how much we need to grow. We can admit to the questions we can't answer. We can get rid of the wax and be who we are, because our ultimate security is not dependent upon any of that. Our security is in God and in God alone. So, we can come into God's presence saying, "Here I am God. This is me. This is the real me."

For years, the invitation hymn for the Billy Graham crusades was, "Just As I Am." Have you listened carefully to the words? "Just as I am, without one plea but that Thy blood was shed for me, and that Thou bidst me come to Thee, O Lamb of God I come. I come." Have you let the meaning of that sink in? When I come to the end of my life and stand before God to give an accounting, my plea will not be, "Receive me God, because I am good. I have done everything I was supposed to do." No, not that. And my plea will not be, "Receive me God, because I am smart. I have all the answers." Not that either. No, my plea will be, "Receive me Father, because I am Your child, one for whom Christ has died, and I have been invited. See, my name is on the invitation. I have been invited, so I have come." That will be my plea, that and nothing else.

I like the conversation that took place between a young boy and the captain of a Mississippi river boat. The boy asked the captain, "How long have you been doing this job?" "Twenty-six years," said the captain. "Wow," said the boy, "you must know where all the rocks are, where all the shoals and the sandbars are." "No," said the captain. "I don't know all of that. But I know where the deep water is."

There are a great many questions I cannot answer. There is much I do not know. But I do know something about God. I have experienced His amazing grace and strength, and that is enough for me!

One final word. During Leonard Bernstein's first year as conductor of the New York Philharmonic Orchestra, one day he was rehearsing the David Diamond symphony. After the rehearsal, Bernstein went to some members of the trombone section and said, "I'm sorry. I think I gave you a wrong cue back there." The musicians were impressed, and later said among themselves, "The idea was that Lenny was not afraid to admit that he might have goofed. Let me tell you, brother. That ain't insecurity. That's security!"

Do you understand? We have to be perfect and all knowing only if we do not have a loving and forgiving heavenly Father. But, in the security of God's love and forgiveness, we can be who we ae and know that we will still be loved. In the security of God's love and forgiveness, we can be Christians without wax!

Prayer: Loving Father, we are grateful that we do not have to pretend in your presence. You know everything about us and yet, miracle of miracles, you love us still. So, help us to live our lives in the security of your love and forgiveness. Save us from phoniness. Keep us from feeling that we must pretend. Take us right where we are and help us to become all that we can be. We ask it in the name of Jesus. Amen.

Born Again

John 3:1-8

Blaise Pascal was a noted philosopher-mathematician who lived in the 17th century. There came a time when he had a sudden, life-changing encounter with God. It was such a dramatic, joyous experience that he wanted never to forget it, never to lose it. So he sat down and attempted to put into words what had happened, how he felt. Then he made copies of his written description and sewed them into the lining of every article of clothing he owned. His testimony was found on his body when he died nine years later. This is how he described it.

> "The year of our Lord, 1654.
> Monday, 23 November,
> from about half past ten
> in the evening until about
> half past twelve at night: fire!
>
> God of Abraham, God of Isaac, God of Jacob,
> not the God of philosophers and scholars,
> Certainty, joy, peace.
> God of Jesus Christ.
> He is only found along the ways that are
> taught in the gospels.

Tears of joy.
I had parted from Him
Let me never be separated
from Him.
Surrender to Jesus Christ."

We have only to hear those words to know that Pascal had experienced something real, something deeply felt. He said it was God. It was more than a new insight or an intellectual discovery, because he was careful to point out that the God of which he wrote was not the God of philosophers and scholars. The word which he used was, "Fire!" Obviously, it was an experience which touched him in his depths and then flooded his entire being. It was an experience which gave him certainty, joy, and peace. And his response to the experience was "surrender to Jesus Christ."

We use a variety of terms to describe what happened to Pascal. We can call it "conversion," "reconciliation with God," being "saved," or we can use the term that Jesus used in our scripture. In that experience, Pascal was "born again."

The expression, "born again," has come into popular usage in recent years, particularly as a variety of celebrities have described themselves as "born-again Christians." But the term has been used rather loosely, in some cases inaccurately, and in too many instances, arrogantly. It's because of the confusion surrounding the expression that I have decided to write about it. Let me get a couple of things straight at the outset. To be born again is simply to be reconciled to God. Jesus might just as easily have said to Nicodemus, "You must experience and accept God's forgiving love." The expression, "born again," is simply another way of saying it. Further, every Christian has been "born again." To speak of "born-again Christians" seems to imply that there are Christians who have not been born again.

In some instances, unfortunately, the term is used arrogantly to suggest that members of certain groups are authentic, genuine Christians, you know, "born again," while people who are not members of that group are somehow illegitimate or counterfeit Christians.

I feel like weeping when I see the prideful ways in which some people try to separate themselves from the rest of God's family. You've heard the terms. "We're a Bible believing Church." "We're a full gospel Church." "We are born-again Christians." All of that seems to imply that the rest of us are not Bible believing, do not experience the fullness of the gospel, and have not been born again.

Let's get one thing straight once and for all: the quality of a person's relationship with God is between that person and God. It is not my place or yours to say who is or who is not an authentic member of God's family. May God have mercy on those people who are so very sure of their own salvation and so very unsure of everyone else's.

Further, if we rightly understand it, the gift of God's grace must not be an occasion for arrogance. If we are loved by God it is never because we have deserved it, but because God has chosen to give it. Therefore, the appropriate response is not pride, but humility, thankfulness, and obedient service.

Now, having said those things preliminarily, I'd like to make three observations about the experience of being "born again."

I.

The first has to do with a closer look at what it means to be "born again." When we go to the Greek language in which

77

the New Testament was originally written, we discover that the term, "born again" has a dual meaning. It does mean "born again," that is, born for a second time. That was what confused Nicodemus. He asked, "Can (a person) enter a second time into his mother's womb and be born?" Of course, that's not what Jesus is talking about. He is talking about a second birth, but a different kind of birth by which we enter the Kingdom of God. Jesus said, "That which is born of flesh is flesh, and that which is born of Spirit is spirit." So, the second birth is the birth of the spirit.

The second meaning of the term we are discussing is, "born from above." Well, that fits in with the idea of spiritual birth doesn't it? Our second, or spiritual birth, is a birth which comes as a gift from God. It is "from above."

Now when Jesus told Nicodemus that he must be "born again," He was not singling Him out. It is quite clear from reading the New Testament that this is an experience which God wants to give to every person. Every human being, in order to be fully human, needs the experience of being born from above.

Let me say again what we mean by that. We can use a variety of expressions to describe it, but every person needs to experience the reality of God. Every person needs to feel the cleansing of God's love and forgiveness. Every person needs to know that he is affirmed by God, that he is a unique, special, valued son or daughter of God. Every person, then, needs the experience of re-orienting his life around its only proper center, who is God. That's the way it needs to be because that's the way God intends it, and nothing else ever works out quite right.

If we are to fulfill the purpose of our creation, each of us must come to that moment when we know that God is God, that we are sons and daughters of God, and that life in relationship with God is therefore good. Something of Pascal's experience, which he described as certainty, joy, (and) peace," must be ours. That moment must come for every person when we know who God is, who we are, and consequently what life is all about.

Morality is not enough. A "good life" is not enough. God wants from us more than a pattern of "good guy" behavior. What God wants from us is a relationship. He wants sons and daughters. That's why we were created. That's what life is all about. And that's why so many people miss the mark by a million miles when they assume that the main point of religion is morality. Those people who say, "I live a good, moral life, why do I need the Church?" just don't understand. God wants more than that. He wants to love us and to be loved by us and then to let that love produce lives worthy of the name "Christian." Don't you see, then, that to be "born again" is to be born into a conscious relationship with God, that relationship for which we were created.

I want to say one more thing about that before I go on to the next point. I believe that it's important to know that we are the sons and daughters of God... not just with our minds, not just with wishful thoughts, but with our entire being. We can know that God is here, that we are loved and forgiven, that we have been born into a new relationship with God. We can know that! There is a good old Methodist word which describes what I am talking about. The word is "assurance." We can know!

Assurance is what Wesley experienced at Aldersgate. He had always understood the Christian faith with his mind, but after Aldersgate he knew. And that got him into trouble. I recall an incident recorded in Wesley's journal. Those staid, reserved Anglicans didn't know exactly how to react to those

79

singing Methodists with their doctrine of assurance. One gentleman was quoted as saying concerning John Wesley: "Why, his impudence we cannot bear. He says he knows his sins are forgiven!" Well, why not? I agree with what Gypsy Smith once observed, "The person who can get religion and not know it can lose it and never miss it!"

Those early Methodists liked to preach from that text in the eight chapter of Romans: "His spirit bears witness with our spirit that we are the sons and daughters of God." To know that, to be certain of that is not impudence or arrogance. Because we are not talking about anything we have done or achieved. We are talking about the gifts of grace which God has given. Without any tinge of pride or arrogance, I can say, "I am a Christian!" Because that is not a claim to goodness or worthiness. It is a celebration of God's love. It is an expression of the fact that, in spite of my unworthiness, God has chosen to love me, forgive me, and give me the gift of new life!

What I am saying is that God intends for every person to be born into a loving, trusting relationship with Himself. To miss that is to miss life, and to experience that is to experience the assurance that we are the sons and daughters of God.

II.

The second observation I'd like to make about being born again is that experience comes to people in an infinite variety of ways. There is no single type of religious experience which can claim exclusive validity. If you want to know one of my pet peeves, it has to do with those people who insist that my religious experience must duplicate theirs in order to be valid.

In a word, that's hogwash! God has created an infinite variety of people. Surely He would not deal with each of us in exactly the same way. History demonstrates that God uses diverse approaches. God is an opportunist, always looking for appropriate ways to reveal Himself and make His ways known. As a result, He is a God of endless surprises. Only dull-witted, unimaginative people would try to put God into a straight-jacket and maintain that God has only one methodology! Fortunately, God is not inhibited by our small minds. His ways of dealing with us are like a man rowing around an island again and again, looking for the best place to land. God is constantly looking for openings in our defenses, opportunities to give us His gift of grace. He works within our freedom. He works with the chances we give Him. That's why there is no single, standard model of Christian experience.

For some, religious experience is sudden, dramatic, emotional. They can name the day and the hour. Such was the experience of Paul on the road to Damascus or of Pascal who expressed it in terms of "Fire!" For others, it is quiet, gradual, almost imperceptible. But the end result is the same. They are both in a loving, growing, serving relationship with God.

During my growing up years, I heard several ministers describe the experience of being "born again" as like the breaking of a horse, the bringing of a horse under the will and control of its master. One horse is broken in the way we have seen in western movies. The owner goes out, puts a bridle and a saddle on it, climbs into the saddle, and rides the hose as it runs and jumps and bucks, trying to throw the rider, until finally, almost exhausted, the horse gives in to the will of its master and is broken. As second horse might have a totally different experience. The first day the owner goes out and talks to him, pats him on the nose, and gives him a lump of sugar. The second day he goes out, puts a bridle on, and gently leads him around the corral. The third day he puts a blanket over the horse and again leads him around. The fourth day he adds a saddle. The fifth day he slowly climbs into the saddle and gently rides around the corral.

Now ask those two horses if they have been broken. The first horse would say, "Yes, I've been broken. I can name the day and the hour. It was a sudden, dramatic, emotional experience." The second horse might say, "I don't know exactly when it happened. It was so gradual, so gentle. But I'm broken. I'm sure of that. I'm broken."

It's true, isn't it. The end result was the same. But the kind of experience was utterly different. Your religious experience doesn't have to be like mine. Perhaps you can't name the day and time. Perhaps you have never had a dramatic, emotional experience. That doesn't necessarily mean that you have never been born again, any more than periodic cases of religious goose bumps means that you have.

The key thing is that, however it happens, the time must come when we know that we have said "Yes" to God. The time must come when we have centered our lives around the reality of God in Christ. We may not know exactly when it began or how it happened, but the time must come when we know that we are a son or daughter, loved, forgiven and affirmed by God. Until that happens, life is incomplete.

III.

One final observation. We can prepare ourselves for the "born again" experience. We can seek to be open to it. We can position ourselves in the channel of God's grace where it is most likely to come to us. We can begin to live by faith, attempting to live each day as if what the Christian faith says is true, anticipating that we will then discover in our own experience that it is true. All of those things we can do to prepare for the experience, but we cannot program it. We cannot say when it will come to us or how it will come to us. The born again experience is a gift of God, never given without our permission and cooperation, but always given when and how God pleases.

Again looking at our text, there is an engaging play on words in the Greek language. The Greek word for "spirit" and "wind" is the same. So, when Jesus is talking to Nicodemus He speaks of being born of the spirit, and then He uses the same word to paint a picture, using the movement of the wind as His imagery. He said, "The wind blows where it wills, and you hear the sound of it, but you do not know where it comes from or where it goes; so it is with everyone who is born of the Spirit."

Do you hear what Jesus is saying? We can never be sure when the wind of God's spirit will choose to blow. He operates according to His timetable and not according to ours. That's when God chooses to give His gift. I try always to remember that it was when John Wesley went unwillingly to a prayer meeting on Aldersgate Street that the wind of God's spirit blew across Wesley's life, and he was never again the same. He wasn't expecting anything, but if he hadn't gone…

For 2000 years Christians have understood the importance of prayer, the reading of Scripture, receiving the sacraments, meeting regularly with the family of God for worship. These are the things we do to prepare ourselves, to place ourselves in the channel through which God's grace has always flowed, to stand on that high hill across which the wind of God's spirit chooses to blow. Then we wait.

We don't know when it will be. We don't know how it will come. But we do believe that if we prepare for it and are open to it, the experience of new birth will come to us as it has come to those before us. God wants us to be born into a loving relationship with Himself. He wants to give us the experience of assurance, of knowing that we are the sons and daughters of God. That's what God wants to give us... our task is to get ready to receive it.

In closing I want to tell you about a man known to many of us who apparently had a religious experience like we've been talking about. His name is Charles Colson, an assistant in the Nixon White House. He named his autobiography, "Born Again."

Colson had always sought out men of power and influence. He made himself subservient to them, hoping to gain advantage by attaching himself to their coattails. He was willing to do virtually anything they asked in order for him to feel important.

But increasingly, Charles Colson became aware of the emptiness of his life. The glitter and glamour of the Washington whirl did not satisfy him as it once did. Then Watergate and all its attendant pressures began to take their toll. He began to feel that his whole world was crumbling and he had nothing solid to grasp.

It was then that he sought out a man named Tom Phillips, a Boston businessman, the president of Raytheon Corporation, and a former acquaintance of Colson's. Phillips had a life-changing religious experience and Colson wanted to know more about it, especially since Phillips was a successful business man and a person whom Colson respected.

So one night Charles Colson made an appointment to visit Phillips at his home. After visiting informally for a while, Colson asked him what had happened. Phillips told him that he had been reading C.S. Lewis' book, "Mere Christianity." He said, "Let me read you a passage from it." And this is what he read:

"There is one vice of which no man in the world is free, which everyone in the world loathes when he sees it in someone else. There is no fault which we are more unconscious of in ourselves, and the more we have it ourselves, the more we dislike it in others. And the vice I am talking about is pride, the concentration on the self."

I am sure that the idea was nothing new to Colson, but at that moment in that situation those words struck him with tremendous power. Those words were describing him and his miserable situation.

After some additional conversation, which saw Charles Colson dodging, rationalizing, evading, but not convincing anyone, least of all himself, Tom read some passages from the Bible, and then offered to pray for Chuck. His prayer was not stilted and formal, but genuine and real. He prayed, "Lord, we pray for Chuck and his family, that You might open his heart and show him the light and the way..."

During the prayer, Chuck began to feel what he later described as a "kind of energy." And then a wave of emotion came over him which almost brought tears. There was so much in him that was crying out for release, but he held it back. After the prayer there were the usual pleasantries. Tom gave Chuck his copy of C.S. Lewis' book to read, then with a hand on his shoulder and a fond farewell, he sent him on his way, not yet a new man, but with the newness beginning to form.

85

Let Charles Colson continue the story in his own words:

"As I drove out of Tom's driveway, the tears were flowing uncontrollably. There were no street lights, no moonlight. The car headlights were flooding illumination before my eyes, but I was crying so hard it was like trying to swim underwater. I pulled to the side of the road not more than a hundred yards from the entrance to Tom's driveway, the tires sinking into soft mounds of pine needles. I remember hoping that Tom and Gert wouldn't hear my sobbing, the only sound other than the chirping of crickets that penetrated the still of the night. With my face cupped in my hands, head leaning forward against the wheel, I forgot about machismo, about pretenses, about fears of being weak. And as I did, I began to experience a wonderful feeling of being released. Then came the strange sensation that water was not only running down my cheeks, but surging through my whole body as well, cleansing and cooling as it went. They weren't tears of sadness and remorse, nor of joy – but somehow, tears of relief. And then I prayed my first real prayer. 'God, I don't know how to find You, but I'm going to try! I'm not much the way I am now, but somehow I want to give myself to You.' I didn't know how to say more, so I repeated over and over the words: Take me. Take me. Take me."

That was a turning point in Charles Colson's life. He became a different man. He started a ministry to prison inmates and worked full time in that program until his death. He said that he was not quite so obsessed with himself, that increasingly God became the center of his life. And he was at peace!

Believe me when I tell you that something like that can happen to you, if it hasn't happened already. It's a gift that God wants to give you. You can experience the reality of

God. You can know that you are a loved, forgiven, affirmed child of God. Whatever your present situation, you can be born again... and that's good news!

Prayer: Come Holy Spirit, come. Come as the wind that cleanses. Come as the fire that refines. Come as the still small voice that assures us that we are sons and daughter of God. Come to us and give us new life in Christ. In his name we pray. Amen.

...And Then Some

Matthew 5:38-48

A retired executive who had been very successful in business was once asked the secret of his success. He said that he could sum it up in the words "...and then some." In explaining his unusual answer, he went on to say, "I discovered at an early age that the difference between average people and the top people was that the top people did what was expected of them ...and then some. They were thoughtful of others, they were considerate ...and then some. They met their obligations and responsibilities fairly and squarely ...and then some."

This executive was using new words to express an old truth, a truth not just about business but about all of life. This truth is one Jesus taught and by which He lived. Jesus would never allow his disciples to be satisfied just to "get by," to be average, mediocre people. He was always challenging them to go beyond that which was required or expected. He said, "What are you doing *more* than others?" He said, in effect, "If you are my followers, you must be characterized by a spirit that goes further and does more than can be reasonably expected." You will remember that the Scribes and the Pharisees were the righteous people, the very best people of Jesus' day. Yet, Jesus said to his followers, "Unless your righteousness exceeds that of the Scribes and Pharisees, you will never enter the Kingdom of Heaven."

Jesus then went on to make sure the disciples understood what He meant. He explained this principle of going further than was required, doing more than was expected, by talking about going the second mile, returning good for evil, loving your enemies. No-one could reasonably expect you to do any of those things, but Jesus insisted that we go beyond minimal expectations, that we do more than anyone would anticipate. And the surprise of that, the shock of that would reveal that something has happened to make us different, something has happened to mark us as followers of Jesus. Jesus said, "So you love those people who love you, do you? So what! That's easy. Everybody does that. That's the easy thing, the expected thing. What I want to know is, what are you doing *more* than others?"

Do you understand what He is saying? He was speaking not just to his disciples in the first century, He was speaking to us 21st century Christians as well. As followers of Jesus, we are to do everything good that others can reasonably expect of us, but not be content with that. We are to do everything good that others can reasonably expect of us …and then some!

Of course, what Jesus asks us as his followers to do is simply to reflect the way God deals with us. God never gives us the bare minimum. God never tries to get by as cheaply as possible. We don't think about it enough, but every moment of every day God gives us abundantly more than anyone has a right to expect. Just think about the way God created the world. This world is filled with lavish gifts from God. Patricia and I were sitting in a nice restaurant recently, enjoying a good meal, and suddenly it hit me. (I suppose that after sixty-two years of marriage she is accustomed to my strange comments that seem to come from nowhere.) In the midst of the meal, I said, "Isn't it great that God has given us the ability to see, and taste, and smell?" It didn't have to be that way, you know. God could have provided for our nutritional needs by giving us a tasteless pill to swallow instead of a rich variety of tasty food. Isn't it great that God planned for us to meet our nutritional needs in such an enjoyable way! I take that as an expression of God's love.

Just think about it. God could have created the whole world in black and white, no color. Instead, just look at creation. God could have made a world without flowers and birds and butterflies and sunsets and stars. He could have made everything flat, without hills and valleys and majestic mountains. God could have made the world without hobbies to pursue, without useful work to do, without loving relationships to enjoy. I could go on and on, but you get the point. God wants us to do more than survive. God wants us to LIVE, and to live abundantly, expansively, enjoyably! Isn't it clear that God gives us more than any of us have any right to expect. And that *more* is one of the strongest evidences of God's love for each of us. God gives us everything that we need ...and then some!

Jesus' life is a good example of what I am writing about. Jesus was constantly astounding people by the extent of his loving and caring. Again and again He went beyond what anyone had a right to expect. No one could expect Him to care about lepers, thieves, prostitutes and tax collectors, but He did. No one could expect Him to welcome the company of all the marginalized outcasts of his time, but He did. No one could expect Him to love a disciple who betrayed him, but He did. No one could reasonably expect Him to forgive his executioners, but He did. And I am convinced that at least part of his greatness is in the fact that Jesus constantly loved more, forgave more, and helped more than anyone had any right to expect. Jesus is the supreme example of the power of those words …and then some.

I know that what I am writing about is not easy and does not come naturally. It is contrary to our inclinations. There is something about most of us that wants to take short cuts and get by as cheaply as possible. I remember the student who was fond of saying, "The way I figure it, "C" is passing, so anything higher than a "C" is just wasted effort!" Most of us have learned to do that which is required of us. It's difficult to pass a course, hold a job, or sustain a marriage if you don't do what is required. So we have learned to do that. But many of us become angry when someone suggests that we do more than our share of the work, carry more than our share of the load, or love someone more than they love us. "Why," we say, "that's not fair. And it's not reasonable!"

I don't think I'm overstating the case. We are very sensitive to the possibility that others will take advantage of us and work us too hard, charge us too much, or respect or love us too little. And when this happens to us, when we discover that indeed someone is violating our rights, a chain reaction tends to take place. We tend to react to others in terms of how they have treated us. We react to anger with more anger. We react to shoving with more shoving. We react to violence with more violence. I suppose that's the normal thing, the expected thing.

But it's not the redemptive thing. Before redemption can come to any situation, before newness and reconciliation can come, someone must stop doing the easy thing, the expected thing, and break the chain reaction by doing the extravagantly loving thing. Jesus described it as turning the other cheek, going the second mile, and returning good for evil. There are marriages that could be made good again if someone would break the chain reaction. Many international tensions could

92

be eased if someone would break the chain reaction. Old feuds could be overcome if someone would break the chain reaction.

That is what Jesus was asking when He told his contemporaries to adopt the practice of going the second mile. Those first century Jews were a conquered people, conquered by the Romans. It was Roman law that a Roman soldier could compel a Jew to serve as his porter and carry his pack up to a mile. It made no difference whether the Jew had urgent business of his own, or was already near exhaustion from heavy toil. He was forced to obey. To a Jew who was proud of his race and heritage, this law was a constant source of humiliation and a persistent reminder that they were living under Roman domination.

You can imagine the shock and anger then, when Jesus told his contemporaries not only to obey this unjust law, but to go beyond it by volunteering to go the second mile, to do more than the law required! Can you imagine! Jesus seems here to be making an unreasonable request. But then, whoever suggested that Jesus only makes reasonable requests! Listen now, I'm about to write something important: to the person who hasn't tried it, this principle of going further and doing more than required, this business of going the second mile and returning good for evil, all that seems absolutely foolish. But to the person who has tried it, to live Jesus' way, doing all that we are required and expected to do …and then some, is the key to abundant life. Let me give you two reasons why.

First, it changes our experience of life for the better. For the person who does what is expected …and then some, life is changed from a burden to a joy, and I don't think that is an exaggeration. Jesus said, "I have come that you may have life, and have it abundantly." (John 10:10) In pursuing the best life, we often want God to change our circumstances, but Jesus gives us abundant life by changing us and our attitudes, and that changes everything! Among other things, He changes us from the kind of person who cuts corners and tries to get by as cheaply as possible, to the kind of person who gives as much as he can to whatever he is doing. It changes everything when we learn to give ourselves unreservedly to life. The principle of ...and then some helps us to do just that.

Let me give you a couple of examples. There was a streetcar conductor who was known for his cheerful and courteous demeanor. A man who was a regular on his route asked him about it one day. The conductor smiled and said, "Well, about five years ago I read in the paper about a man who was included in a will just because he was polite. 'What the heck,' I thought, 'it might happen to me.' So, I started treating passengers like people, each one important. And you know what? It makes me feel so good that now I don't care whether or not I am remembered in a will!'" His situation, his circumstances were not changed at all. *He* was changed. But his change in attitude really changed everything else. It was the principle of doing everything that was expected ...and then some, at work.

Harry Emerson Fosdick, that outstanding preacher of a former generation talked about it. He told of the time his mother sent him out to pick some berries. She told him to pick a whole quart that day. He was reluctant and somewhat resentful as he started out. That was not how he had planned to spend his day. The sun was hot, the insects were numerous, and it seemed that the thorns all found a way to prick his hands. But suddenly it occurred to him that it would be a good thing to surprise his mother and pick twice as many berries as she had asked him to do. Fosdick said that as soon as he made that decision, the whole experience was changed completely, from a task to a joy, from a burden to an adventure. Everything was different, he said, because *he* was different, and he never forgot that lesson.

Every person has to decide what to do with, how to feel about what life puts before us. To accept what is given and to do *more* than is required transforms everything. It makes life adventurous and abundant!

But there is a second reason why this way of living is so important. Not only does it make life good for us, it also releases that power that can make other people new. If there is anything I have learned in my life it is that the most powerfully redemptive force in all the world is love. Not just any kind of what we call love, but love that loves enough to give itself at great cost, love that loves enough to suffer for the one who is loved. Wherever in this world there is new life, wherever there is redemption, it is because someone has loved like that.

Of course, you can't communicate that kind of love if you are giving only that which is required or expected, if you are meeting mere minimum standards. No, the redemptive power of this kind of love is released only when there is the shock of love that goes beyond anything that can be reasonably expected. But when you have that kind of love, love that goes the second mile, love that forgives seventy times seven, love that returns good for evil, when you have extravagant, limitless love that never quits, then you have the possibility of newness, and peoples' lives can be redeemed. It's a matter of passing on to others the redemptive love we have received from God. That kind of love makes newness possible and leads to what Jesus called abundant life.

Do you know the name, Russell Conwell? Russell Conwell was a Captain in the Union Army during the Civil

95

War. He was a handsome, well educated man, who had as his orderly a small, fragile man by the name of John Ring. John Ring was totally devoted to his Captain, whom he thought to be everything he would like to be, but was not. One morning there was a sudden attack by the enemy, causing a retreat by Conwell's men. They crossed a river, setting fire to the bridge to slow down the enemy pursuit, leaving behind their tents and equipment. In his haste, Conwell had left his sword, and it was a matter of dishonor for an officer to lose his sword. So, with no thought of his own safety, John Ring rushed back across the burning bridge to get the sword and save the honor of his Captain. By the time he began his return, the bridge was a burning mass. When he was halfway across, the bridge collapsed, and he was caught in the burning timbers. His fellow soldiers went to get him but he was mortally wounded. As soon as he regained consciousness, he reached anxiously for the sword which his buddies had left there beside him. He hugged the sword to his breast and died. No one reasonably could have expected him to go back for the sword, but he did it because of his devotion to his Captain. And the story doesn't end there.

Conwell said, "When I stood over his body and realized that had died for love of me, I made a vow that I would live thereafter, not only my own life, but also the life of John Ring, that it might not be lost." From that day on, when Conwell gave time in service to others, he considered that the life of John Ring. Each day he would work eight hours for himself and eight hours for John Ring, reaching out and meeting the needs of others. He soon found that he enjoyed the hours working for John Ring so much more than the hours he spent working for himself, so he gave more and more hours to John Ring, and finally all of his time and energy was spent in the service of others. He gave a lecture over six thousand times, a lecture he named, "Acres of Diamonds." With that lecture, he made more than a million dollars, quite a sum for that day. He became the founder of a hospital and a university and lived a remarkably influential and helpful life. But, in retrospect, it all happened because of John Ring, who dared to do that which was expected …and then some.

Of course, the best example of what I am talking about is God. You might expect God to love good people, but who would expect God to love sinful, unworthy people? You might expect God to give us a second or third chance to become faithful people, but who would expect God to forgive seventy times seven? Who would expect God to reach out to us in Jesus? Who would expect God to give that ultimate gift at the cross? Talk about going the second mile, talk about returning good for evil, talk about loving your enemies, God has done all of that. The Christian gospel reveals a God who does everything anyone could expect …and then some! And it is precisely because God loves us with that kind of love that we have a chance for newness! And that's the gospel!

Let me say it one more time. It was a time of war, and there was a cartoon in the newspaper that gripped attention. A soldier was driving a jeep across a battlefield with a wounded buddy in the back. Bullets were whizzing by on all sides. Bombs were exploding all around. The scene made you wonder about the outcome. The suspense was alleviated by the caption beneath, saying, "P.S. They made it!" But the thing that really got my attention was the title given to this drawing. Spread across the top of the drawing, in bold, black letters were the words, "Magnificent Fool!"

For the life of me, I can't think of a better title for a Christian. "Magnificent Fool!" Because when you come right down to it, it's foolish to go a second mile when you are only required to go one. It's foolish to forgive seventy times seven.

It's foolish to return good for evil and to love your enemies. It's foolish! But those of us who have tried it have learned that it's a magnificent kind of foolishness! It's the kind of foolishness that makes Jesus worth following. It's the kind of foolishness that makes the Christian life worth living.

Listen to Jesus: 'Unless your righteousness exceeds that of the Scribes and Pharisees, you will never enter the Kingdom of Heaven. What are you doing more than others?" It is my prayer than we will be able to reply, "Lord, I have done everything I have been expected to do ...and then some!"

Prayer: Father, give us that spirit that does not count the cost or measure the distance, but is always ready to go farther and to do more than can be reasonably expected. Help us now, in love, to spend ourselves generously for you and for others. We pray in the name of Jesus, who lived abundantly because He loved extravagantly. Amen.

The Good Shepherd

Luke 15:1-7

We don't know a great deal about sheep and shepherds these days because they are not a part of our daily experience. Probably, most of what we know about them we have learned from the Bible. Sheep and shepherds are an important part of the Biblical story, and I like what I have learned about them there!

God, of course, was the first to be called "the Good Shepherd." The beloved 23rd Psalm begins, "The Lord is my shepherd, I shall not want." When, in their history, the Jews began to have kings, the kings of Israel were said to be the shepherds of the people, and the people were their flock. Jesus referred to himself as "the Good Shepherd." And, when Jesus was born, the news was first announced to "shepherds abiding in the field, keeping watch over their flock by night." One of my favorite pictures of Jesus is the one depicting Him as a shepherd, with a lamb held tenderly on his shoulders. If you read the Bible at all, you can't miss it: sheep and shepherds are found throughout its pages.

And, even our language today is drawn from it. We speak of "Christian congregations." The word, "congregation" comes from the Latin word, "grex," which means "flock." And, the word, "Pastor," means "Shepherd." There is no title in this world I would rather claim and deserve than the title, "Pastor – Shepherd."

Some of the most beautiful and insightful language about shepherds and sheep is found in the gospel of John, chapter 10. There Jesus says, "I am the good shepherd. The good shepherd lays down his life for the sheep. The hired hand, who is not the shepherd…sees the wolf coming and leaves the sheep and runs away – and the wolf snatches them and scatters them. The hired hand runs away because a hired hand does not care for the sheep. I am the good shepherd. I know my own and my own know me…I lay down my life for the sheep." Earlier in the chapter Jesus says that He knows his sheep by name. The sheep know his voice and they follow the shepherd because they trust him. It's a beautiful picture of a caring, trusting relationship between the shepherd and his sheep.

As Jesus tells his parable of the lost sheep in the gospel of Luke, the first hearers were the Scribes and the Pharisees, and they didn't like it very much. There in Luke, chapter 15, there are three parables about the lost. First there is the lost sheep. Then there is the lost coin. Then there is the lost son, the prodigal, and his lost elder brother. All of them are about God's love for those who are lost, loving them so much that He goes out seeking them. Jesus makes the point over and over again. I wonder, why is Jesus so insistent? No doubt Jesus wants to make sure that we understand how much He cares about those who are lost. Jesus tells these parables to explain why He was spending so much time with the lost.

I said that the first hearers, the Scribes and the Pharisees did not like these parables. They had been grumbling about the fact that Jesus was not spending much time with them, the obviously better, more righteous people. Instead, Jesus was spending most of his time with common people, the "am ha-eretz," the "people of the land," those who were not so meticulous about keeping all the details of the Jewish law. Jesus spent time not only with the common people, but even with obvious sinners: the thieves, prostitutes, and tax collectors. So, the righteous people – or, should I say "self-righteous people" – were grumbling and saying, "This man welcomes sinners, and *eats* with them." According to their law, you were not supposed to have *any* dealings with sinners, much less an intimate association like a meal. The good, righteous people just didn't do that with those who didn't merit their friendship.

The Scribes and Pharisees lumped them all together and dismissed them as "sinners." Instead of rejoicing when one sinner was reclaimed, they would more likely rejoice when a sinner was rebuked or destroyed. They looked forward not to the saving of sinners, but to the destruction of sinners. Sinners did not belong to "us." Sinners were "them."

By contrast, look at how Jesus described them. In his eyes they were lost sheep, those He knew by name. And He cared so much for them that He was not willing for even one of them to be lost. He was willing to lay down his life for them! Tell me, is your heart more like Jesus' heart of compassion, or more like the Scribes' and Pharisees' hearts of condemnation. The answer to that question will tell you a lot about whose fold you live in. Hard heart? Or loving, melted heart?

Let's look at the parable more closely. In Jesus' world, most villages would put their sheep together, and several shepherds would take them out to find pasture. The sheep would nibble here, then nibble there, not paying much attention to where the nibbling was taking them. Sometimes, separated from the flock and the shepherd, they would become vulnerable to predators like wolves. Or, sometimes they would find themselves out on a ledge or in a hole from which they could not extricate themselves. They would begin to bleat and the shepherd would go and use his shepherd's staff to bring them up to safety. When it was time to go back to the fold for the night, the shepherd would call out, "mannah, mannah," and the sheep would recognize his voice and follow. Dogs are able to find their way home by themselves, but not sheep. Sheep need a shepherd.

Sometimes a sheep would wander off and become separated – it would be lost. As the day came to its end, the other shepherds would take the rest of the sheep back to the village while one shepherd would go off in search of the one lost sheep. The shepherds who returned to the village would report that a sheep was lost and that his shepherd had gone to find it. And the whole village would stay up, waiting anxiously for word. And when the shepherd returned, especially when he returned with the lost sheep safely carried on his shoulders, the whole village would erupt in celebration! Isn't that a beautiful picture? Jesus said that there is rejoicing like that in heaven whenever a person who has been lost is found. Do you hear the good news in that? God Himself rejoices when one who is lost is found and brought back home again!

In that ancient world in which the village or the tribe or the nation was everything, and the individual counting for very little, do you understand what a revolutionary and wonderful thing Jesus was saying? Ninety-nine percent is not good enough. Every person is important to God, even those who are sinners, even those who are the poorest of the poor, even those the world dismisses as unimportant, God knows by name, and is willing to lay down his life to save them! God will not sleep as long as any of his sheep is lost. Wow! That is inexpressibly good news!

I have said repeatedly in sermons and in teaching that, unless we see ourselves there, the Bible can never be God's word for us. So, do you see yourself in this parable from the gospel of Luke? Are you, or have you ever been lost? I have, and it's not a good place to be.

It's reassuring to me that, in the gospels, Jesus seldom calls people "sinners." Instead, He calls them "lost." They are like sheep without a shepherd. What a suggestive word that is! The sheep were not so much bad as they were careless, inattentive, and distracted. They would nibble here and nibble there, not watching where they were going, and after a time, they discovered that they were lost. What that means is that they were out of right relationship with the shepherd and separated from the rest of the flock. Lost.

I say it again and again: life is about relationships: relationship with God, with ourselves, and with others, and the quality of life is dependent upon the quality of those relationships. If those relationships are not right, we are lost. We may be lost and not even know it. The world is full of people who sense that something is not quite right. They think that if they just keep doing what they are doing, it will all come together soon. Just as soon as we get the next promotion...just as soon as we get out of debt...just as soon as we move into the new house...just as soon as the children are out on their own...just as soon as we have saved enough to retire...just over the next hill we will find greener grass. So, we just keep on nibbling, far away from the shepherd – lost – but we don't even know it.

Or, maybe we *do* know it, or we suspect it, but we hope that if we just ignore it, it will go away. We keep our lostness to ourselves. We keep up appearances. But in reality, who are we kidding? Jesus knows a lost sheep when He sees one. Maybe you are lost in a bad relationship. Maybe you are lost in bad habits of mind, or soul, or body. Maybe you are lost in guilt over what you have done or failed to do. Maybe you are lost in anger or resentment. Maybe you are just tired – experiencing the exhaustion of daily care. Maybe you are weighted down by anxiety about the future. Or, maybe you are lost because you think you are self-sufficient and have no need of a shepherd. Whatever our lostness, the traditional prayer of confession expresses it: "We have erred and strayed from your ways, like lost sheep."

I don't know your condition at this moment, but God does. What I do know is that hope begins when we acknowledge the truth about ourselves and admit our need. That was where hope began for the tax collector praying in the Temple. That was where hope began for the prodigal who "came to himself." And, that's where hope can begin for us. Like lost sheep, we might be in a hole we can't get out of, or out on a precipice in danger of falling. If that's where we find ourselves, maybe the thing to do is to make small noises, like bleating, giving off signals of our location and our condition – something like prayer. Because we can be certain that the good shepherd is not far away. And, as soon as we acknowledge our need of him, He finds us, He loves us, He takes us home where we belong, and there we can live the rest of our lives in his fold under the watchful care of the good shepherd. Remarkably, we discover that God and all the company of heaven is rejoicing because the lost has been found!

When times are tough, instinctively we turn to the 23rd Psalm, don't we? We read it and let it sink deeply into our consciousness, because we need the assurance that everything is okay. We need to know of the shepherd's love, and that He is always with us. Once we have been found and lifted onto the shoulders of the good shepherd, it's a good idea to keep repeating, "Thou art with me...Thou art with me...Thou art with me." We keep repeating that until we really believe it, because it makes all the difference!

Several times I have talked about the rejoicing of the shepherd and the rejoicing in heaven whenever a lost person is found and brought back home again. But what about the joy of the person who was lost? When we are found and are safely in the arms of the good shepherd, there are no words large enough to express our joy! Now we know who we are: we are sheep of his fold. We know whose we are: we belong to the good shepherd. And we know what life is all about: we are to listen to his voice and follow wherever He leads. We trust Him to lead us to green pastures, to lead us beside still waters, and, if we should fall, we trust Him to be there to restore us again. Surely goodness and mercy shall follow us all the days of our life. And then, we shall dwell in the house of the Lord forever. How can you talk about that and know the truth of that without being overcome with joy? Joy! Joy! We were lost, but now we are found! Joy!

I like the way an anonymous poet expressed it:

> "O little black sheep that strayed away, done lost in the wind and the rain,
> And the shepherd, He say, 'O hireling, go and find my sheep again',
> But the hireling say, 'O shepherd, that sheep am black and bad!'
> But the shepherd, He smile like that little black sheep was the onliest lamb He had.
> So the shepherd go out in the darkness, where the night was cold and bleak,
> And that little black sheep, He find it, and lay it against his cheek.
> And the hireling say, 'O shepherd, don't bring that lamb to me!'

105

But the shepherd, He smile and He pulled it close.
And that little black sheep was me."

Joy! Thanks be to God!

Prayer: Thank you Father for never abandoning us, for never giving up on us, for always loving us and seeking us. We thank you that we can never outrun your love for us. We can never exhaust your patience with us. Help us finally to stop running away, so that you can find us, claim us, and restore us to your fold, where we can be loved and blessed forever. Thank you for being our good shepherd! In Jesus' name we pray. Amen.

When Mountains Are Not Moved

Mark 11:22-24, Matthew 26:39

The story appeared in a news release from United Press International. A young man over a period of two years wrote seven hundred love letters to his girlfriend proposing marriage. His persistence finally brought results. A newspaper reported the girl's engagement to the mailman who faithfully delivered all the letters.

Life is often like that, isn't it? We want something so badly we can taste it. We dream about it, pray for it, work to get it, but it doesn't come. We all know the disappointment of that, don't we? The disappointment of dreams unfulfilled... of prayers unanswered.

Perhaps we hoped for a promotion and it was given to someone else. We wanted to pass a test and we flunked. We expected a happy marriage and it ended in divorce. We asked for health and we became ill. We prayed for a loved one to recover from an illness and they died.

It's true. Some prayers are not answered, at least not in the way we hoped. And that harsh reality gives more problems to more people than almost anything I know... especially when we read the words of Jesus recorded in Mark's gospel. Jesus says, "Have faith in God. I tell you this:

107

if anyone says to this mountain, 'Be lifted from your place and hurled into the sea,' and has no inward doubts but believes that what he says will come to pass, it will be done for him. I tell you, then, whatever you ask in prayer, believe that you have received it and it will be yours."

I.

To begin with, I would suggest that we take another look at what prayer is all about. If we are overly troubled by the fact that what we prayed for has not materialized, that may be an indication that we have misunderstood the nature of prayer.

It is true that we are told in scripture to make our requests known to God. And I do believe in the power of prayer. But that doesn't mean that everything we pray for will come to be. It won't. No matter how earnestly, how repeatedly we pray, there will still be disappointments. The fact is, there is no way to structure life to insure that what we want to happen will happen. There will be times in every person's life when it will seem that our prayers have not been answered... when the mountains we prayed to be removed stubbornly refuse to budge an inch.

That is the way it is. But that should not upset us unduly unless we begin with a distorted understanding of prayer. All too many people think of prayer as a means of manipulating God. They instruct, He produces. They have a vending machine view of the universe – insert a prayer and you get a candy bar (or any other goodie which you pray for.) According to that understanding of prayer, God is reduced to the status of a cosmic errand boy, and the philosophy becomes, "not Thy will, but mine be done."

No, that understanding of prayer is a great many sizes too small. It doesn't measure up to Christian standards. After all, God is God. God is not some celestial servant who caters to our every whim. As a loving Father, God graciously invites us to make our requests known to Him. God will grant those requests if they are possible and if they are consistent with His will, but God will not be manipulated like some puppet on a string!

I said that God will grant our requests if they are possible and if they are consistent with His will. That is an awfully big statement and confusing as well. There are so many variables in life. And there is so much complexity that we will never begin to understand. But we have got to try, so here goes.

Often our prayers are not answered in ways that we intend because of the freedom God has granted to all His children. If we pray for something which requires the destruction of someone else's freedom of choice, that is something which God will not do. Life loses its meaning if we become puppets rather than persons, so God will not take away our freedom. He will call to us, plead with us, inspire us, persuade us, but He will not coerce us. If our prayers require that, the answer will be "no."

Similarly I do not believe that God will suspend natural law in answer to prayer. If we fall off a precipice, the law of gravity will not be repealed, no matter how fervently we pray. What kind of world would this be if laws were capricious and undependable? I believe that prayer can work with natural law in ways that we may not understand. But if your prayer requires the suspension of natural law, you are probably going to be disappointed.

Also, we should not overlook the obvious. Sometimes our prayers are not answered because what we pray for is not in keeping with God's will. God is far wiser than we. I have had many occasions to be glad that God did not answer my prayer in the way I had hoped. A minister friend of mine in Mississippi expressed the idea graphically in a bit of free verse. He said:

> "I am not discouraged if my prayers go unanswered; if some were, I would have grave reservations about the sanity of God."

Let's be thankful that God often says, "no." That is one way He has of expressing his love for us.

Let us take another look at our scripture. We often run into difficulty if we take a given scripture literally when the writer did not intend it that way. In the first century Jewish culture, "moving mountains" was a figure of speech which mean, "removing difficulty." So I interpret that to mean: through prayer, through faith, any difficulty in life can be removed – or, if not removed, at least we can be given what we need to cope with it so that it is not experienced as a defeating difficulty. I do not interpret it to mean that whatever I ask for I will get.

That interpretation makes sense, particularly when we see the scripture in the larger context of the entire New Testament. Let us let Jesus teach us about authentic prayer. There are two phrases in Jesus' prayer in the Garden of Gethsemane which leap out at me. First, He prays, "If it is possible, let this cup pass from me." Jesus recognizes that some things are not possible. He has no magical view of prayer. He is under no illusion that all He has to do is pray and it will be done. Still He prays. He makes His requests known to God.

The second phrase in Jesus' prayer is always the bottom line for Jesus. He concludes His prayer by saying, "Nevertheless, not my will, but yours be done." Jesus did not see prayer as a means of bending God's will to His. Just the opposite. As Augustine once said, "When a man in a boat throws a rope to a rock, his purpose is not to pull the rock to the boat, but to pull the boat to the rock." Thus the primary purpose of prayer is not to pull God's will to ours, but to pull ours to God's.

If we will always remember those two phrases, it will save us a great deal of disillusionment with our prayers: "If it is possible," and "Nevertheless, not my will, but yours be done." If we keep that firmly in our minds, we will be able to pray believing that we will receive – if not what we want – at least what we need.

II.

I said at the beginning that we have all known the disappointment of dreams unfulfilled, of prayers unanswered. The second thing I would like for us to consider is: what do we do when mountains are not moved? There is always the danger that we will so concentrate on our disappointments that we will miss our new opportunities. There is a beautiful, hopeful line spoken by Maria in "The Sound of Music." She says, "When God closes a door, He always opens a window." I believe that. I believe that God is always working in our behalf for good.

Let me say by way of clarification that often a door is closed not by God's intention, but by His reluctant permission. I believe that often when we are disappointed, hurt, or grieving, God enters into those feelings too, and shares them with us. God regrets the difficult, hurting experiences of life as much as we do. But I do believe that

111

Maria is right. Whatever reason the door is shut, God immediately sets about the task of opening a new door or window. God refuses to be defeated, and He does not want us to be defeated either. No matter what painful thing occurs, God immediately goes to work to bring something good out of the evil. That is what God does because He cares about us so. He loves us.

The problem is that we cannot go through the new door that God opens if we are concentrating our full attention on the door that is closed.

There are so many wounded people walking around who are not getting well because they keep picking at the scabs of past hurts. It is a sad thing to be hurt... disappointed... wounded. We have all experienced that to some extent. To be human is to be hurt. It is always sad to see someone who has tripped and fallen in life. But I will tell you what is really tragic. The most tragic thing of all is for someone to trip and fall and then refuse to get up again.

Something happens to hurt them and from that time on they can see nothing other than their hurt. They spend their life rehearsing their tragedy again and again. They feel sorry for themselves. They accuse others for their hurt. They blame God. That is the saddest thing of all – they are so preoccupied with their disappointment that they fail to see the possibilities of new life. They die long before their hearts stop beating.

Consequently, they miss the gospel. Because the good news is that God loves us. No matter what disappointment we have encountered, no matter what hurt we have experienced, God is at work to bring something good out of that. One of my favorite Bible verses assures us that "God works in all things for the good with them that love Him."

The amazing thing is that so often the new door which God opens may be far better than the old one we wanted so much.

If we will open our eyes in faith we will discover that God's love is at work in our behalf. We will find open doors that we never saw before. We will be able to affirm prayers that have been answered and dreams that have been fulfilled. Life will still be full and good. I like the way one poet expressed it:

> "I've dreamed many dreams that never came true,
> I've seen them vanish at dawn,
> But I've realized enough of my dreams, thank God,
> To make me want to dream on.
>
> I've prayed many prayers when no answer came
> Though I waited patient and long,
> But answers have come to enough of my prayers
> To make me keep praying on.
>
> I've trusted many a friend who failed,
> And left me to weep alone,
> But I've found enough of my friends true blue
> To make me keep trusting on.
>
> I've sown many seeds that fell by the way
> For the birds to feed upon,
> But I've held enough golden sheaves in my hands
> To make me keep sowing on.
>
> I've drained the cup of disappointment and pain
> And gone many days without song,
> But I've sipped enough nectar from the roses of life,
> To make me want to live on."

That is a good word. There is more to life than disappointment and unanswered prayer. If we will open our eyes of faith we can see it. A good and loving God will make life good for us if we will give Him the chance!

III.

That leads us into the final thing I want to say, and that is that in spite of our disappointments we must continue to trust in God's love and providence. That is the only way. If we can't trust in that, then I confess that I don't know what we can trust.

When disappointments come, when hurts are experienced, we are tempted to quit on prayer, to give up on God. How many people do you know who stopped praying because something they prayed for never came to be. They say, "I've tried prayer, and it doesn't work." Or, how many people do you know who have lost whatever faith they once had because God allowed some painful experience to come to them.

Of course, that's the test. That is the acid test of authentic faith. It is no problem to have faith in God when every prayer is answered... when we are miraculously delivered from every difficulty... when we are rewarded for our faith by being healthy, wealthy, wise, and happy. No, faith is no problem whatsoever under such circumstances.

The question is, what do we do when our prayers are not answered, when the mountains are not moved, when in spite of our best efforts and earnest prayers the difficulties of life threaten to overwhelm us. Is God still God for us then? Do we still trust Him then?

That is what faith is all about. It is believing in, trusting in, placing our full weight upon God, even when we are hurting, even when there are questions we can't answer, even when it is dark and we can't see the light. Even then faith affirms: God is loving and powerful. He will not let us down. I will place my trust in Him!

That is the kind of faith we see again and again in the scriptures and it is never misplaced faith. There is Job, everything he values in his life is taken from him, he is afflicted with boils, he is sitting there in the ash heap trying to figure it all out. Someone counsels him, "Curse God and die." But even though he doesn't understand it all and even though his pain remains, he comes forth with a magnificent statement of faith: "Though He slay me, yet will I trust in Him."

There were those three Hebrews: Shadrach, Meshach, and Abednego, being sentenced to the fiery furnace because of their refusal to bow down to idols. Listen to their statement of faith: "Our God whom we serve is able to deliver us... and He will deliver us out of your hand, O King, But if not, be it known to you, O King, that we will not serve your gods, nor worship the golden image which you have set up." Do you hear it? Even if God did not deliver them, He was still their God!

There was the Apostle Paul, praying numerous times to "have the thorn in his flesh removed." In a sense, his prayer was unanswered because his thorn remained. But in a larger sense, his prayer was answered. God said to him, "My grace is sufficient for you." And Paul found it to be so.

Then there was Jesus. He did not want to die at such a young age. He prayed about it: "Father, if it is possible, let this cup pass from me." In just a few moments after praying that prayer, He was in the hands of His executioners. His experience of pain and desolation was so great that He said from the cross, "My God, my God, why have you forsaken me?" But even that cry was directed to God, the Father. And His final words were, "Father, into your hands I commend my spirit."

What these people asked for sometimes was not given. But what they needed was always provided... through faith. We may as well admit it, prayers are not always answered in the way we hope. Mountains are not always moved. But as long as God is God, we are not alone, and we can cope. Listen to the good news: "My grace is sufficient for you."

Prayer: Father we are grateful for prayers which are answered, for Your sustaining love which is with us when what we want is not possible or not wise. Father, do not let our disappointment obscure our future possibilities. But help us to trust in Your loving providence to bring something good out of whatever raw material life provides. We make our prayer in faith that You are God, and that Your grace is sufficient for our every need. In the Master's name we pray. Amen.

Overheard in a Barber Shop

John 9:1-3; Romans 8:28

Normally I'm not much of an eavesdropper. I believe that people's private conversations should be just that... private. But one day, while I was seated in a barber chair, minding my own business, there was a conversation between the man in the chair next to me and his barber. I could not help hearing what they said.

They were talking about a woman who was a mutual friend. And they were agonizing over her misfortunes. First her husband had left her with two small children. He had refused to make child-support payments, so she was working and struggling to make ends meet. Not only was she trying to overcome the hurt which comes from being rejected, it was all she could do to stay alive. She literally did not know where the next meal was coming from. And to top it all off, she had gone to the doctor the week before and had just learned that she had cancer. That was too much. No one could deserve all of that. The man in the chair concluded the conversation by saying, half jokingly and half angrily, "It makes you wonder if someone up there doesn't like her!"

Those two men would never have stated it so classically, but what they were talking about was the ancient problem of evil. Why does life include the possibility, even the probability that we will be badly hurt? If God is good, why do we have a world in which so many people suffer?

I.

That's the question the disciples were raising in the scripture. There was a man who was born blind and they wanted to know why. They assumed that his suffering was the result of someone's sin, so they asked, "Who sinned, this man or his parents?" That's usually the assumption we make. If we are good, then good things will happen to us. If we are bad, then bad things will happen to us. God pays off or God punishes depending upon what we deserve. There is some truth to that, but it is far too simplistic. It's a dangerous generalization, no matter how popular it is.

Do you remember that delightful scene in the "Sound of Music" in which Maria and Captain Von Trapp are in the garden, their hearts pounding with the excitement of love? They began to sing to one another. "Here you are standing there loving me, whether or not you should; and somewhere in my youth or childhood, I must have done something good." That may be a good lyric, but it's bad theology.

Yet, that's the popular explanation. Something good happens, so it must be a reward for good behavior. Something bad happens, so it must be punishment for bad behavior. So goes the popular wisdom.

Of course, as I have said, there is some truth to that. I would have to agree that most suffering is the result of sins that we or others have committed or errors that we or others have made. We live in a world of laws and those laws have consequences. When we violate a natural law, that law will work to our destruction just as dependably as it works to our benefit when we cooperate with it. Similarly, when we violate a moral law, someone will suffer the results of that. To be sure, we can be forgiven and cut free from the guilt of sin, but consequences remain.

I can understand that kind of cause and effect suffering. If we violate a law, we will have to endure the consequences. And no matter how painful, I can understand that and accept that. I would not want to live in a capricious undependable universe in which God is constantly suspending first this law and that in order to spare us from hurt. In such a world we would not know what to count on. And the emotional impact of such uncertainty would probably be even greater than our present suffering.

One thing I think it is important to understand is that God does not want his children to suffer. I'm sure of that. Whatever suffering there is is by God's reluctant permission, and not by His intent. I believe that the hurts which come to us as a result of our choices are all tied up with the laws by which our world operates and with our freedom to make choices. And please hear this, I am convinced that the overwhelming majority of hurts which come to us are the direct consequences of our choices, or the choices of others.

Let me give you some examples of what I mean. Many people think that if you transact a business deal dishonestly God might punish you in the future by causing you to fall and break a leg or by making you have an automobile accident. I believe that such fuzzy thinking is only slightly short of pagan superstition. What does breaking your leg have to do with a dishonest business deal? They are totally unrelated events. One has nothing to do with the other.

That doesn't mean that you can be dishonest and get off scot free. It does mean that the consequences will be related to the offense. A dishonest business deal might result in being arrested, or in losing a good reputation, or losing your own self-respect, or suffering the torments of a guilty conscience, or insomnia or indigestion or a thousand and one other possible consequences… but all related to the sin which was committed.

Again, if you commit adultery, you will not be struck by a thunderbolt. Then again, you might be, but not as a consequence of the unfaithfulness. They are unrelated. But there will be consequences because there is a moral law and there is a righteous God. "God is not mocked. Whatever you sow, you reap." But in this case what you will reap will more probably be a strained relationship with the one you have wronged, a lowered self-image, guilt feelings, maybe even divorce. But the consequences are related to the deed.

I wish we Christians could get this straight once and for all. God's love for us, His goodness toward us is in no way dependent upon our behavior. Jesus said quite clearly that God "makes His sun rise on the evil and on the good, and sends rain on the just and on the unjust." We badly misunderstand if we think that God gives special favors to those He deems to be worthy of them, and withholds favors or even punishes those He deems to be unworthy. No, you can never understand evil and suffering on such a simplistic basis. The scriptures declare that God loves all people equally, the moral and the immoral, the caring and the careless, the faithful and the faithless. God is for us all and He wants only good for us all. God takes no pleasure in human suffering.

But there are laws at work. When we cooperate with them, life is mostly good. When we violate them, someone is hurt. That's the price of freedom. That's the result of having our choices mean something. I am convinced that even that kind of suffering is not what God intends. No loving human father would ever want His children to suffer. Neither would

God. I believe that painful, difficult experiences happen with God's reluctant permission. And I believe that such things happen not with God's intention, but as the logical consequence of our choices. A couple of examples: A small boy came to dinner one night and found a dish with two prunes in it next to his plate. He knew they were for him and he didn't like prunes. His mother said, "Tommy, eat your prunes." "No," Tommy replied. "Prunes are good for you, eat them." "No." "Eat them, Tommy." "No, I won't." "Tommy, God won't like it one bit if you do not eat those prunes." Tommy sat silently and defiantly. The mother lost her control and began to shout: "Thomas Allen, either you eat those prunes right now or you can march up the stairs to your room and stay there."

Sullenly, Tommy went to his room, while his mother worked in the kitchen downstairs. As soon as Tommy walked into his room, a sudden summer thunderstorm came rolling into the community. The skies were dark and menacing. Lightning was flashing all around. Loud, rolling claps of thunder were shaking the entire house! The mother became concerned about little Tommy, alone in his room in the face of such a storm. She went running up the stairs, into his room just in time to see him with his elbows propped on the window sill, looking out at the storm, and muttering aloud, "Gee whiz, God! Such a lot of fuss about two little prunes!"

Of course, there was no connection. One was not a consequence of the other. And yet, so many of us are equally as sloppy in our theology as we try to connect disconnected events and try to attribute them to God's judgment, or God's punishment. I just don't believe that is the way God works.

I heard a very wise man say a number of years ago: "We are rewarded not so much *for* keeping the commandments, as *in* keeping them." Similarly, we are punished not so much for breaking the commandments as in breaking them. The deed and the resulting consequence are connected. It's the law of sowing and reaping at work. You plant a flower and you reap a flower. You sow a weed and you reap a weed. If you refuse to eat your prunes your mother might punish you, you might not have proper nutrition, you might even be constipated... those are all reasonable effects of the original cause. But God won't throw a storm at you. There is no connection. That's superstition.

Another example: I don't know whether or not this story is true, but it is funny in a macabre sort of way. A man was up on his roof repairing the shingles. To keep from sliding off a very steep roof, he tied a rope around his waist, threw the other end over the peak of the roof and down the other side to the driveway asking his son to tie it to something good and solid. The son saw the family car sitting in the driveway, so he tied the rope to the bumper of the car. Everything was working quite well until the son left to play ball and the mother came out to go shopping. Unaware of her husband's brilliant plan, she pulled out of the driveway with her husband soaring over the peak of the roof.

Why did that happen? Was he being punished because of some past sin? Of course not. That's not the way God works. That mishap occurred because the father gave instructions without checking out the details, because the son was short-sighted and careless, and because the wife failed to see the rope tied to her bumper. After all of that, the laws of physics and the law of gravity operated as they always do, dependably, even when we are hurt as a result.

You can understand that kind of suffering and so can I. It's the result of our sinful choices or our ignorance or our carelessness or simply, our bad luck. There are natural and moral laws at work. Even though we don't like it, we can understand it. It's the result of human decisions, and that explains the overwhelming majority of human hurts.

II.

But, having said that, I must go on to say that still there is a sizable body of human suffering that I cannot explain, and I have been wrestling with it all of my life. I started writing papers about it in high school. I continued through college and graduate school. Here I am writing about it, and yet I still have no satisfactory answer. I don't understand the evil which comes to us without any human choice being involved. I don't understand massive freaks of nature which swoop down and kill thousands of innocent people in one blow. I don't understand why some children die in childbirth. I don't understand why there is leukemia and cancer and heart disease. I just don't understand.

I have heard all of the clichés. "God sends evil in order to punish." "God makes us suffer in order to help us grow." "God called this person because He needed him in heaven." If those ideas are comforting to you and you can believe them, so be it. But they don't ring true to me. I have no better explanation. I simply say that some suffering goes beyond our ability to understand. And I know that one of the first things I want to do in heaven is to ask of lot of "why" questions.

In the meanwhile, there are some things I continue to believe. I believe that, obviously, there is suffering that is not related to our sin or our error. It's not all punishment. It just happens and I don't know why. I believe that God never intends suffering for His children. Certainly once it occurs God can use it to help us grow, to help produce depth of character. He can work with us to bring something good out of it. But I don't believe He intends it. He wants good for us, just as all of us parents want good for our children.

In fact, I will even go a step further and say that I believe that when we are hurt, when we do suffer, God suffers along with us. He shares our sorrows. He enters into our suffering. You know, that's a relatively new idea in the history of religion. In ancient times, people conceived of God as aloof, removed from the daily grit and grime of human life. But in Christ we have come to see God as One who is intimately involved in our daily joys and sorrows. He really cares. He hurts when we hurt. He weeps when we weep. I believe that there is something healing about that, something redemptive in that.

So, I say again, there is much evil and suffering that I can't explain, but I believe that God does not intend it. He only reluctantly permits it. And once it occurs, He regrets it as much as we, and in His great Father's love, He shares our suffering with us.

Two parents, suddenly and prematurely, lost their only son in an automobile accident. They accused God, angrily saying, "Where is God now?" The answer came back, gently but firmly, "He is exactly where He was when His own Son died. And He is doing the same thing, grieving."

III.

I know I have not given you an explanation of all evil. I have no such explanation to give. But I suspect that in the darkest nights of the human spirit, we need not so much an explanation as a solution. The basic question is not, "Why?" But, once evil occurs, how are we to answer it? How are we to overcome it? That's what we need to know.

I take great comfort in the fact that Jesus never said, "I have explained the world." He said, "I have overcome the world." That's what we need. Let's get back to our original scripture. When the disciples asked Him about the man born blind, Jesus was not interested in relating the misfortune to anyone's sin. Nor was the practical Jesus particularly concerned about any explanation. His compassion caused Him to look for a solution. He said, "Let's see what God can do with it." And He healed him.

That's Jesus' approach. Let's not dwell on explanations, because sometimes explanations are hard to come by. Besides what we really need is a solution. So, let's see what God can do with it. We Christians need to understand what God's promise to us really is. It is not that we are exempt from trouble. It is not that we will be spared all suffering. No, that's not the promise. We must come to understand that the promise is that God loves, He cares, and He is always with us, and at every moment is at work for our good!

The promise is that nothing can separate us from the love of God... nothing! The promise is that "In everything God works for good with those who love Him!"

Don't you hear the hope in that? No matter what misfortune has befallen us. God cares, and He immediately begins to work to bring something good out of the situation.

Two of the most significant days of the Church year are Good Friday and Easter. Those two events have a lot to do with what I am talking about. I don't believe for a moment that God wanted Jesus to die on the cross. I believe that God wanted people to respond to Jesus, to say "Yes" to Him, to become faithful disciples of Jesus. He didn't want His Son to die such a brutal, humiliating death. That crucifixion was history's most heinous crime. Of course, God knew our

125

sinful ways well enough to know it would probably happen and He permitted it to happen rather than to intervene and destroy our freedom to choose. I have to say that God permitted it even though He didn't intend it. But once it occurred, God took that evil event and turned it into mankind's greatest blessing. He brought something fantastically good out of it. He turned the crucifixion into a resurrection, because that's the kind of God He is! He is always working to bring good out of evil. And that's good news!

Let's conclude where we began. Do you remember the woman they discussed in the barber shop? Well, I don't believe for a moment that her difficulties were the result of someone up there not liking her. And they were not the result of her being punished for her sins, at least not in the sense of God intending for those things to happen to her. Some of her troubles were understandable consequences of human choices. The divorce, the missed child-support payments, the struggling to make ends meet, the sense of rejection are all the painful results of someone's choices. The cancer I can't explain. But I am sure that it wasn't punishment and I am convinced that it was nothing that God intended.

What she needed was not an explanation, but a solution. Perhaps she needed a helping hand from some of her friends. She needed to know that she was not alone, that nothing could separate her from the love of God. And she needed to hear as we all do, those strengthening, reassuring words, "In everything God works for good with those who love Him." "Remember, I am with you always, even to the end of the world."

If I believe anything, I believe that. And I also believe that, finally, that is the only solution there is to the problem of evil.

126

Prayer: Father, when we are at our best we don't want explanations as much as we want solutions to the problems of life. We are grateful that You love us and that You want only the best for us. We celebrate the realization that You are with us and that nothing can separate us from Your love. So come to us now, Father, and give us what we need. Heal us. Strengthen us. Reassure us. For we pray in the name of Christ, our Lord. Amen.

Crossing the Jordan

I Thessalonians 4:13-18

Turn through the pages of the Bible and you will find occasion after occasion when words alone are not enough. In seeking to probe the mysteries of life, in seeking to affirm the great truths of life, no words are large enough. So, repeatedly, we find writers of scripture painting pictures of the truth. After all, we have heard all our lives that "one picture is worth a thousand words."

For the most part, Jesus taught in parables, which are really word pictures, more easily understood and remembered than words alone. When God wanted to reveal himself, no word description was adequate. People had tried for thousands of years to capture the nature of God in words, and some words do help. But the fullest revelation of God awaited a picture: "The word became flesh and lived among us." (John 1:14) It is in Jesus' life, death, and resurrection that we see the best, the most complete, the most beautiful picture of God. So, I repeat: the profound mysteries of life, the great truths of life demand more than words. Nothing less than a picture will do.

And, what greater mystery is there than the mystery of death? What greater truth can be affirmed than eternal life, life beyond death? What words can we choose that will deal adequately with such an important reality? It's true, isn't it, words are not enough. Descriptions alone are not enough. Somehow we must *sense* the truth. We must see with our eyes and feel with our hearts as well as hear with our ears. It is not surprising then that we are most helped by the *pictures* of life and death that we find in the Bible.

Our experience tells us that, sooner or later, in one way or another, everyone dies. Our life on this earth comes to an end, either because of accident, or illness, or old age. But, the ageless question is, what happens then? Is death the end, or is there more?

The Bible answers that important question by painting pictures. One of the pictures is drawn from one of the dominant events of the Hebrew Bible, the Exodus. You will remember that Abraham, the father of the Jews, was called by God to leave his homeland for a new land which God would show him. So, he and his family left the security of the known and began their journey to an unknown land, a land they believed God had promised. Generations later, the Jews wound up as slaves in Egypt. God called Moses to go to Pharoah to say, "Let my people go!" After a prolonged struggle, Pharoah capitulated and released them. They continued their long and difficult journey toward their new land, with God leading them on their way. That journey is what we call "The Exodus." Moses never got there with them, but he saw the land of promise from afar, from Mount Nebo. Shortly after Moses' death, the Jews crossed the Jordan River and entered the new land, the land they had dreamed about, sought after, and struggled to reach. Finally, they thought, they were home!

That became, for Christians, a beautiful picture of what death is like. Death is like crossing the Jordan River. When we cross the river we do not disappear into nothingness. No, we cross the river and enter that land that has been prepared for us, that land that has been promised to us. Heaven is our promised land. And, of course, as we Christians see the picture, the promised land is not an unexplored land. Jesus has gone on ahead of us, as He promised, "I go to prepare a place for you. And if I go and prepare a place for you, I will come again and receive you to myself, that where I am, there you may be also." (John 14:3)

Paul is talking about the same thing in the scripture from I Thessalonians. Paul is talking there about the imminent return of Christ. He says that those who have already died have gone to join Christ in heaven. And then, the rest of us will be welcomed there when we die. Christ himself will greet us personally and take us home, to our eternal home, to our promised land. There God will be with us, there God will "wipe every tear from our eyes, and death will be no more; mourning and crying and pain will be no more." (Revelation 21:4) That is the beautiful picture painted in the Bible. That is the promise of scripture.

When you look across the river, the river of death, what do you see? There are a great many people who see nothing. Of course, they are devastated by the reality of death, and they have my compassion. It takes a special kind of seeing to see across the Jordan. It takes the eyes of faith. Spirituals have always painted marvelous pictures of what we can see with eyes of faith when we look across the river. Do you remember?

"Deep river. My home is over Jordan.
Deep river, Lord, I want to cross over into camp ground."

It is a picture of our promised land. And there is this one,

131

"I looked over Jordan and what did I see,
coming for to carry me home?
A band of angels coming after me,
coming for to carry me home."

While I'm writing about the time of slavery in this country and about how the slaves were comforted and strengthened by thoughts of heaven, I have to acknowledge not only their faith, but also their wisdom reflected in the spirituals. They knew that the injustices and hurts of this life would not be continued in the next. God would see to it! Here, in this life, the plantation owners and their families had shoes and the slaves did not. So they sang,

'I got shoes, you got shoes, all God's chillun' got shoes.
When I get to heaven, gonna put on my shoes,
gonna walk all over God's heaven!'

And, usually slaves had to eat leftovers after the owners had eaten. Clearly, they were second class people, not deserving of anything better. So, in singing about heaven, they sang,

"I'm gonna eat at the welcome table one of these days!"

Sadly, some slave owners tried to use religion and talking about what awaited the faithful in heaven to try to make slaves more content with the unjust conditions they endured here. But the slaves were wiser than they knew. While they sang about putting on their shoes in heaven, they also sang,

"Everybody talking 'bout heaven ain't going there!"

They knew that in God's heaven wrongs would be righted and hurts would be healed. Things would be the way they are supposed to be!

Something like that is what death is like when we see it through the eyes of Christian faith. It's crossing the river into the promised land, to be with God, to be with loved ones who have crossed the river before us, to be there at home, our eternal home. That's a beautiful picture!

Either that picture is an accurate one, or as far as I am concerned, nothing in life makes any sense at all. I think about the family members and the friends who have crossed the river before us. Every one of them is a unique and unrepeatable miracle of God's loving and creative power. Why would God create them, encourage them to develop their minds, their abilities, their interests, allow them to enter into loving, caring relationships, only then to allow them to disappear into nothingness through what we call death? Why indeed? That wouldn't make any sense. Isn't there something deep within each of us that cries out against the insanity of that? I agree with Robert Millikan that, "The divine architect of the universe has not built a staircase that leads nowhere." Of course He hasn't!

Years ago, a Harvard professor, Professor Palmer, lost his wife in death. At a young age, while full of life, a germ went to work, a tiny little germ, and she died. In his grief, Professor Palmer wrote, "Who can fail to sense the irrationality of the universe if, out of deference to a few particles of disordered matter, it excludes so fair a spirit!"

I believe that if death is the final word about us, if the world is nothing but an endless cemetery, then the universe *is* irrational, and I, for one, rebuke it and the God who made it. I want no part of such a world, a world in which the best is ever at the mercy of the worst, and life is ever overcome with death. I want no part of it!

But, thank God, that's not the way it is when we see with the eyes of faith. When we people of faith look over Jordan, we see more. And what we see assures us that the universe is not irrational. The best in life is not at the mercy of the worst, because the final word about us is not defeat, but victory! Seeing with eyes of faith, we can say along with Paul, "O grave, where is your victory? O death, where is your sting? ... Thanks be to God who gives us the victory through our Lord, Jesus Christ." (I Corinthians 15:54-57) The final word about us is not death, but life. When we look over Jordan, we see more!

When we affirm such things, how do we know that we are not just running away from the painful reality of death? How do we know it is not just wishful thinking?

For one thing, our instincts tell us so. In every culture, in every generation throughout history, people have longed for life after death. Throughout the world, we have discovered tombs equipped with all that people would need in life after death. It is instinctive, and for every other instinctive longing there is a corresponding reality. I believe God placed that longing deep within us as God's promise of that which is to come. As the eminent physicist, Blaise Pascal, said so profoundly, "When God wants to carry a point with his children, He plants it deeper than the mind, in the instinct." Of course. There it is in all of us, this longing for continuation. And the more we love, the more we feel it. God put it there. It's God's promise to us. Instinct.

Second, when I look at the God who revealed himself in Jesus, a God of love, of goodness, and of power, I know that death cannot be the end. If God is like Jesus, God will not leave us in the grave. I put my trust in that. I trust in the character of God, as He has made himself known in Jesus. When I come to my own death, I will not trust in my goodness to give me hope of eternal life. I will not trust in my achievements, or even the amount of faith I have. I will place my trust in the character of God as revealed in Jesus. John Greenleaf Whittier has said it beautifully in what has become my favorite poem:

"Within the maddening maze of things, and tossed by
    storm and flood,
To one fixed trust my spirit clings, I know that God
    is good.
I know not what the future hath of marvel or
    surprise,
Assured alone that life and death, his mercy underlies.
I know not where his islands lift their fronded palms
    in air,
I only know I cannot drift beyond his love and care."

That is where I place my trust, and where I invite you to place your trust, in the character of God as revealed in Jesus, the Christ. If God is like that, there is life beyond death!

Most importantly, and this is the third thing, we know the truth of eternal life because of the resurrection of Jesus. The scriptures tell us that Jesus rose from the grave as the "first fruits" of those who slept. That is the way the Bible speaks of death. Paul said to the Thessalonians, "I would not have you to be uninformed, brethren, concerning those who are asleep." That's another one of the pictures: to die is to go to sleep. And, of course, we know that when we go to sleep, we wake up. The Bible says that Jesus was the first one to wake up, and because He has awakened, we too will awaken. Because He has conquered death, we too shall conquer death. Jesus said, "Because I live, you too shall live!" (John 14:19) We know the truth of eternal life because of the resurrection of Jesus. Whether we are facing our own death, or whether we are struggling over the deaths of those we love, we need to hear and to believe the reassuring good news of eternal life.

But that does not mean that we are not to grieve. Of course we are to grieve. Nothing about our belief in life after death should deny the reality of our grief or the appropriateness of our grief. Our love gives us the right to grieve. Almost invariably, when I conduct funeral services, I say that our grief is the other side of our love. If we had not loved so much, we would not now hurt so much. If there had not been so much joy in life, there would not be so much pain in death. So I would not want to reduce the pain of our grief by any degree, because the only way to do that is to reduce the love and the joy, and that is too high a price to pay. As a part of our grief perhaps we will shed tears, and that is good. That's one way we have to express our love. But, as we shed our tears, let's understand that we are weeping for ourselves, for our sense of loss. We are not weeping for the ones who have crossed the river, because they have already reached their promised land. They have already inherited that special place prepared for them by Christ.

And, although they have crossed the river, even before we experience our own crossing, I believe that we can have a continuing relationship with our loved ones. I believe that in a real sense, they are always with us. Often I sense my parents' presence. I can feel their love. I can sense their encouragement and support. So, if there is any unfinished business, if there are things you wish you had said or done, but didn't, it's not too late. I believe they know. I believe they understand. I believe that in a real sense they are here, even though they have crossed the river. That is what we are getting at when we say in our communion liturgy: "With angels and archangels, and with all the company of heaven, we laud and magnify your glorious name." The writer of Hebrews says it: "Seeing that we are surrounded by so great a cloud of witnesses..." (Hebrews 12:1) The cloud of witnesses is the company of people who have crossed the river, but who are still with us in a real sense. Do you understand? Wherever we are, and especially when we gather with people of faith in worship, we are in the loving presence of those who have crossed the river.

So, we grieve. Even though they are still with us in a real sense, we miss the way it was before. We miss being able to see them and to hold them. We grieve in that sense, and that's okay. But we Christians do not grieve like those without faith. Paul says, "I would not have you grieve as others who have no hope." (I Thessalonians 4:13) The bottom line of our faith is hope and trust. So, we don't grieve like those without faith. Even in the midst of our pain, even through the blurred vision of our tears, we still hope. We can still see across the Jordan. We can see all the way to our eternal home!

I've been saying that the deepest truths of life can be communicated best through pictures. I believe that, so let the final word be a picture.

Years ago, John Todd was pastor of the First Congregational Church of Pittsfield, Massachusetts. His aunt, who had been like a mother to him when his mother died, became seriously ill, and was frightened about death. So, she wrote to this much loved minister/nephew and shared her apprehension, asking some questions about death. This is what he said in reply:

"It's been thirty-five years since I, as a little boy of six, was left alone in this world. You sent word to me that you would give me a new home, that you would be a mother to me. I have never forgotten that day when I made the long journey to your house in North Killingsworth. I can still recall

137

my disappointment that, instead of you coming for me, you sent your servant in your stead. I can still remember the tears in my eyes, and my anxiety, as I started toward your home with that servant. It was night, and as the darkness deepened, I became more frightened. I asked, "Do you think she will go to bed before we get there?" "O no," he answered, "she'll wait up for you. When we get to the next clearing, you'll see the light in her window." Presently we did ride into the clearing and I could see the light in her window. And I remember that you were waiting at the door to greet us. And you put your arms around me, and you took me into your kitchen and fed me. And after supper you took me up to my new room, heard me say my prayers, and sat beside me until I fell asleep. You undoubtedly realize why I am recalling these things to your mind. Someday soon God may send to take you to your new home. But don't fear the summons, or the journey, or the messenger. Because at the end of the road you will find love and a warm welcome waiting. God can be trusted to be as kind to you as you were to me."

Isn't that a beautiful picture? "You will find love and a warm welcome waiting." That is death seen through the eyes of faith. Death is not disappearing into nothingness. No, death is crossing the river and being welcomed home!

Prayer: Loving Father, we thank you for the lives of those we love who have gone before us into death. We are grateful for the privilege of knowing them and loving them. We are grateful for the memories we hold dear and for the example which is our heritage. And, above all, we are grateful for the assurance of eternal life in Christ. We entrust to your loving care all those who have crossed the river. Care for them until the time of reunion, when we cross the river and are welcomed into our promised land, our eternal home. In Jesus' name we pray. Amen.

The Promise of Wholeness

Revelation 21:1-4

I believe in life after death. If I believe anything I believe that human life does not disappear into nothingness at the grave. Across twenty centuries Christians have been saying that death is not a time when life ceases, but a time when the form of life changes. At birth we come from God. At death we return to God. We enter into that place prepared for us and we live eternally in our Father's house.

When someone we love has died, it is an experience of such loss, such pain, such desolation, that when we are able to affirm a belief in life after death, that comes as an experience of unutterable joy. It is an experience of joy precisely because it comes over against such profound sadness. When we begin to believe, really believe, that the final word about us is not death, but life, then we feel like breaking into song. Indeed Christians have often sung joyfully about our victory over death.

There is the last verse to that favorite hymn, "Amazing Grace." "When we've been there 10,000 years, bright, shining as the sun; we've no less days to sing God's praise than when we first begun."

Then there is the hymn which John Wesley quoted on his deathbed: "I'll praise my maker while I've breath, and when my eyes are closed in death, praise shall employ my nobler powers. My days of praise shall ne're be past, while life or thought or being last, or (while) immortality endures."

It's important for us to talk about this because however persistently we repress it, the reality of death will not go away. So I repeat: With all my being, I believe in life after death. As far as I am concerned, nothing in life makes any sense at all if death is allowed to ring down the curtain on our existence. But my belief in eternal life is not mere wishful thinking. There are at least three reasons why I believe it.

First, my instinct affirms it. Deep within each of us there is a longing for life after death. For every other universal human longing, there is a corresponding reality. Why should this be the exception? I like what Blaise Pascal once said: "When God wants to carry a point with His children, He plants it deeper than the mind, in the instinct." Well, there it is, this deep longing for continuation. And the more we love, the more we feel it. I believe that the one who put it there is God. That's the first reason I believe. My instinct tells me there is life beyond life!

Second, I believe in life after death because of my experiences with God. In my life I have experienced God to be a God of love, forgiveness, and power. I believe that that kind of God would not call us into being, encourage us to develop our minds, our talents, our personalities, inspire us to enter into deeply meaningful loving relationships only to allow all of that to disappear into nothingness through what we call death. No, I agree with Harry Emerson Fosdick when he says, "God is not some crazy artist who goes around painting pictures only to erase them" No, if God is loving and forgiving and powerful... in other words, if He is like

140

Jesus, then He can be trusted to make loving provisions for his children. Just as I would not tolerate the extinction of one of my children, so we believe our heavenly Father will not tolerate the extinction of one of His.

Finally, I believe in life after death because of the promise of scripture. Again and again, the Bible tells us to trust in God, to prepare for the life to come. Jesus Himself said, "Because I live, you too shall live." Especially in the resurrection, we are assured of our victory over death. So, if the scriptures are at all trustworthy, we know that for us death will not mean cessation, but transition... transition to eternal life in our Father's house.

As I write about eternal life, about the promise of wholeness in the life to come, I don't want to be misunderstood. Often Christians are reluctant to talk of eternal life because of the irresponsible or excessive talk which is often associated with it. There are people who tell more than they know and who encourage pre-occupation with the next life to the exclusion of this.

I don't want to be guilty on either count. I freely admit that there is much about the life to come which I don't know. I will have a lot of questions to ask when I get there. Also, we must never become so concerned with the life to come that we fail to live fully and faithfully in the present. I believe that, rightly understood, belief in eternal life can give us such hope and assurance that we can be delivered from anxiety and grief and set free to live fully and authentically and helpfully in the now.

Besides, if we are faithful to the gospel we must affirm our belief in eternal life. That's a part of our good news, and it's something each of us desperately needs to hear. So, I want to tell you some things I believe about the life to come.

Again, I will not speak in much detail (and I suggest that you become properly skeptical when someone claims to know more than he can know.) After all, the scriptures say, "Eye has not seen nor ear heard, neither has it entered the heart of man the things that God has prepared for those who love Him." In the final analysis, I'm content with that. I'm willing to trust a loving heavenly Father to prepare something good for us. And the fact is, there are only some things we are capable of understanding. We are so locked in to our categories of space and time that we find it impossible to think in other terms. I believe that eternal life will be so completely different from our present experience that there is much we could not possibly understand. Still, I do believe that some helpful things can be said... they are these:

I.

First, I believe that eternal life will involve a wholeness of relationship. For years I have believed that we only confuse ourselves when we speak of heaven and hell as places. That's our spacial thinking again. I like to speak of heaven and hell not so much in terms of places as in terms of relationships. To be separated from God... to be out of relationship with God is to be in hell. To know the joy of God's presence, to be with Him in relationship is to be in heaven. So, along with me, think of eternal life in relational terms.

When Paul wrote about the resurrection, he talked about the resurrection of the body. He was not thinking of our physical bodies, however. He was talking about our personhood... that which makes us who and what we are. He believed, and I believe, that as whole persons we live beyond the experience of death. We can know other people and be known. We can enter into loving relationships with God and with family and friends. I can't conceive of any heaven

142

worthy of the name that did not provide for reunion with those we love.

There are a number of people at this very moment whose lives have been scarred and spirits numbed and joy diminished because death has separated them from those they love. I believe that for us death will be a time of reunion with those who have gone before. It can be a time of joy for us because of the broken relationships that are restored.

Jesus spoke of life after death in relational terms. You will remember that He said to the thief on the cross, "Today you shall be in paradise." In large measure, being with Him, is what makes it paradise. Relationship.

John, writing in the book of Revelation, says it too. As he tells of his vision of the new Jerusalem, the holy city of God, which is his term for eternal life, he says a great voice spoke from the throne of God saying, "Behold, the dwelling of God is with men. He will dwell with them, and they shall be His people, and God himself will be with them." Relationship.

I have often said that when I get to heaven I want to ask a number of questions, many of them "why" questions. I am anxious to visit with many of the pioneers of faith who went before us to prepare the way. But there is something personal, too. I have a sister whom I have never met. Imogene was the firstborn of my parents and she died while still an infant. I was not born until some fifteen or sixteen years later. I have never come to know and love my sister. But I will. Eternal life will be a time when that broken relationship will be made whole.

That's something all of us can celebrate. If you have not yet suffered loss through death, you will. The good news is that the loss is not permanent, it is temporary. Eternal life is a time of renewed relationships. I believe that it is a time of wholeness in relationship.

II.

The second thing I believe about eternal life is that it will be a time of growth toward wholeness of personhood. Although I am not at all sure what form eternal life will take, I am utterly convinced that the experience will not be static, but dynamic.

Some of our images of life in our Father's house are totally inadequate. Pearly gates and golden streets and a city in which people live in ivory palaces, a place where people lie around on clouds all day, that is, when they are not strumming on their harps or going to choir practice... that's not heaven to me. And I can't imagine some of the heroes of Church history being very comfortable in such a place. Rough, tough, blustery Peter, the activist, the go-getter... that playboy turned saint, Augustine... the swaggering, sometimes earthy and profane, but always dynamic and energetic Martin Luther... that tireless and fiery horseman, John Wesley... I can't imagine any of them being content for long to lie around in perpetual ease.

No, there will be work to do, projects to complete, growing to accomplish. Our images are totally inadequate, but I am convinced that life in the Kingdom of God must be dynamic and not static.

It must be like that. Because I am sure that even if I live out to a ripe old age. I still will not be finished with the task of growing into all that Jim McCormick can be. There will be talents undeveloped, opportunities neglected, experiences missed. There will still be some things about me I won't like.

144

I expect to have more time in which to allow God to shape my life. I expect to spend eternity loving and being loved, and allowing that love to call forth from me all that I can become.

Do you hear the good news in that? We don't have to complete the project here. We've just got to start in the right direction and make earnest progress. I do believe that in our future life there will be time for growth toward wholeness of personhood.

III.

One final thing. I believe that in the coming Kingdom, wrongs will be righted, hurts healed, limitations removed! In those senses it will be an experience of the wholeness of life.

We have only to look around us to know that not everything in this life is fair. It just isn't. There are people who seem never to have a fair chance at life. There are those who have a lot of luck, most of it bad. There are infants who die in childbirth, youth who are killed in accidents, adults whose lives are cut off long before they complete their three score years and ten. It seems that so many die before they have a chance to live. And a great many of the people who live long lives never seem to have a chance at the good life God intends for all His children.

Honesty demands that we admit that for so many people life is not fair! If we believe that God is good and loving, if we believe that the minimum due every person is justice, then there has got to be a time when wrongs are righted, when injustices are compensated for, when whatever burdens that have kept us from a full experience of life are lifted. That's another reason I must believe in life after death. I believe that God is just. That's why there's got to be more to come.

Years ago, when our nation was in its infancy, slaves used to sing about it. Often the slaves would cook the dinner and wait on the table and then stand back meekly while their masters ate. They would have the leftovers to eat later. Of course, the best food was always gone. They had the backs and wings and necks of chickens again and again. It was a constant reminder of their second class status. And it was unfair.

You can understand why, when they dreamed of the eternal city of God, they sang, "I'm going to eat at the welcome table one of these days." So many things are wrong here, but they will be righted there. The justice of God demands it.

Don't misunderstand. We don't affirm this belief in order to make us satisfied with present injustice. Just the opposite. Our belief in eternal life gives us hope and strength. It enables us to believe in a just and good God. Fortified with such faith, we are able to combat present injustices and, as far as is humanly possible, to make wrongs right, here and now!

As a Pastor, I often see people whom life has not treated fairly. They may have crippled bodies, undeveloped minds, scarred relationships. I see such people and I feel like weeping because I know how painful life must be for them. But then my faith enables me to rejoice, because I know that the way it is now is not the way it will always be! Wrongs will be righted, hurts will be healed, and limitations will be removed.

As I say these things, I can't help thinking of Olive Benesch. Olive was a long time church member and friend who for years had a severe hearing loss. It became so bad that she was virtually without hearing and had to depend heavily on lip reading for communication. Olive was one of my

146

favorite people. She was an example of rare courage and remarkable faithfulness. In spite of the fact that she couldn't hear and in spite of the fact that in the church sanctuary she was too far away to read lips, Olive continued to participate in worship every Sunday. She understood worship far better than most. Authentic worship does not depend primarily upon "what you get out of it," but upon what you bring to it. Even though she could not hear, there was something Olive wanted to say by her attendance – she wanted to declare her faith – she wanted to announce her identity. She was a child of God, saved by grace, and the way you say that is by worship! So she came, not to listen, but to say something with her life. And say something she did!

Still, I am sure that she longed to hear the hymns and anthems sung, the prayers prayed, the scriptures read and the sermons preached. As far as I can tell, Olive was the very first one to order a volume of my printed sermons. That touched me. Because it said to me that she was anxious to read that which she had been unable to hear. The book was paid for, I inscribed it to her, but she never picked it up. She died in her sleep and was found lying peacefully in bed one Sunday morning.

I believe that, as surely as there is a God in heaven, Olive's hearing has been restored. She has been made whole. We do not take our weaknesses and our limitations into our Father's house.

David Ireland used to talk about it. David was in a wheelchair, paralyzed from the neck down, He wrote a book about his life experiences. In his book he tells of times when he dreamed and saw himself in heaven. But he never saw himself in heaven as a cripple. There his health was restored. He was released from his wheelchair prison and he walked and ran and leaped!

That's the vision of one of our most loved hymns:

> Hear Him, ye deaf, His praise, ye dumb,
> Your loosened tongues employ;
> Ye blind, behold your Savior come,
> And leap, ye lame, for joy!"

That's the promise. The good news is that in whatever ways life has been incomplete, unfair, painful, or broken, in God's Kingdom all of that will be past history. Life will be whole. Life will be good. The promise is that "God will wipe away every tear from their eyes, and death shall be no more, neither shall there be mourning nor crying nor pain anymore, for the former things have passed away." That's the promise. Wholeness!

Prayer: Father, we are grateful that because of Your love for us You have promised us the gift of eternal life. Help us to believe in Your promise. And because of Your promise free us to live fully, authentically, joyfully in the present. For we pray in the name of Christ who came to love us and to save us, and who has gone now to prepare a place for us. Amen.

Conviction With Compassion

John 8:3-11

You and I are living today in the midst of a massive moral muddle. There is a pervasive confusion concerning what is right and wrong. And people in increasing numbers are beginning to wonder whether or not such terms should even be used. After all, we have been told again and again that all values are relative, that standards of behavior change from generation to generation. We have seen it happen that an action which is declared unacceptable in one decade is approved in the next.

So, people throughout our land are beginning to believe that there is no fixed point on the moral compass. Morality, indeed, is only a scare word intended to frighten and inhibit. We are an enlightened people, so let us free ourselves from outdated and old-fashioned ideas. The watchword of our generation is freedom! Broad-mindedness! Our mottos are, "Do your thing!" "Grab all the gusto you can, you only go around once!" "Live for the moment!" "If it feels good, do it!"

Increasingly, that's the spirit of our time. Whereas the people of former generations were fearful of the consequences of immoral behavior, that's not our fear. Most of us are not fearful of consequences. We're most fearful of being called, "narrow minded" or "old-fashioned." Almost above all things, we want to be liberated, up-to-date, "with it."

I wish I could celebrate such an attitude. At one level I'd like to join the mass migration into a liberated, uninhibited, permissive future. I don't enjoy being out of step with the majority. And I certainly don't like to be called, "old-fashioned." But at some points I am. I have to be, because as a Pastor, I see where our moral confusion is taking us. Every day I am called upon to help straighten out the wreckage of someone's life. And all too often the hurt has been caused because someone began to believe that what history has taught us about right and wrong is somehow no longer acceptable. They discover too late that, contrary to the popular wisdom, God's moral laws have not been repealed, and that what a person sows, he reaps. What I see as I move among hurting people is that in so many cases our vaunted liberation is not really freeing, that our broad-mindedness does not lead to a larger experience of life, and that taking down all the moral sign posts does not help people to go where they really want to go. There are altogether too many people who are wandering around in confusion. Our culture has told them that they will be happy if they will discard their inhibitions and do as they please. So, they bought that. They tried that. But they are not happy. And I believe that they number in the millions.

It is such a serious problem that I want to write about it, using the scripture in the gospel of John as our point of reference. The questions are: How do we regain morality without becoming moralistic? How do we make moral judgments without being judgmental? How do we let people know that we love them no matter what their behavior, without at the same time giving approval to behavior that is unacceptable? Let's look at the way Jesus did it.

I.

The first thing we can see as we look at Jesus' encounter with the woman accused of adultery is that He made a moral judgment. She had sinned. Her behavior was unacceptable and so Jesus condemned her behavior. Jesus' love for her did not require that He pretend her sin did not exist. In fact, just the opposite was true. It was precisely because He did love her that He had to identify and condemn the behavior that was hurting her.

You know, we make so many serious mistakes in the name of love!.. like the unwise parents who, in the name of love, give and cater and coddle... they always say "yes" and never say "no"... they always give and never demand... there is total freedom and no restraint... and what is produced is a spoiled, self-centered, irresponsible, unhappy person, ill-equipped for life in the real world. In the name of love, so many people are twisted and hurt.

I wish we could learn once and for all that love is not weak. It is not wishy-washy. Authentic love is strong! It gives, but knows the healthy limits of giving. It does not accept unacceptable behavior. Oh, to be sure, it does not require acceptable behavior as a condition of love. It goes on loving no matter what and it grants freedom even to do destructive things. But it cares what decisions are made. And it dares to say, "You are wrong. You made a mistake. You created a hurt," when such words are appropriate.

I believe that we have to make moral judgments. We must bring ourselves to say, "This is good. This is evil." Without such judgments there can be no responsibility, no accountability, and therefore, no virtue. Don't you see, life becomes meaningless if one course of action is as good as any other.

151

I choose to believe that, morally speaking, everything is not up for grabs. I believe that there is behavior that God applauds and behavior that God deplores. I believe that there are paths that lead to life and others that lead to hurt and heartbreak. I believe that it remains true today as it has been true for generations that it is better to tell the truth than to lie... that it is better to be honest than dishonest... that industry is preferable to laziness... that faithfulness is better than infidelity... that moderation is better than excess... that humility is preferable to arrogance... to care about others is better than indifference... to extend a helping hand is better than living as if it's every man for himself... to forgive is better than to accuse... and to love is better than to hate.

I choose to believe that all of that is true. I don't believe that there is anything unique about our generation which cancels out what history has told us to be good and true and life giving. I have seen too many people discover all too late, amid their tears, that morality is not a matter of indifference. There is a way that leads to life and a way that leads to destruction.

It's not good news to me for someone to say that there is no such thing as good or evil; that it doesn't, therefore, make any difference what I do. Don't you see, if my behavior is a matter of indifference, then my life is a matter of indifference. I can choose anything, live any old way and it doesn't matter. That's not good news. That's bad news. It's saying that my life doesn't count. And that's what we human beings fear more than anything else.

The good news is that this is God's world. God created us to live in relationship with Him... in a loving obedient relationship with Him. God calls us to the highest possible standards of behavior. And He cares what we decide to do. There is a great deal at stake in the decisions we make.

Don't you see, that means our lives count for something, because God Himself cares what we do! That doesn't mean that He will stop loving us if we make the wrong decision. But it does mean that He cares about what we do with our lives.

We Christians must get over the notion that because God's love is unconditional, it therefore doesn't make any difference how we live our lives. That's nonsense. Of course it makes a difference. We are called upon to rediscover our moral directions — to take those directions from Christ and not from our prevailing culture — and then to begin living according to the highest possible standards. There should be something distinctive about Christians! We should not blend easily and comfortably into the confusion of the prevailing moral backdrop.

Roy Larson talks about persons who describe themselves as "Christians incognito." "Sometimes (that is, most of the time)," he says, "I think their disguise is altogether too effective. It makes me wonder, is it a disguise? I think particularly of some I know who try to imitate Hugh Hefner and St. Francis of Assisi at the same time. After all, they both like bunnies, don't they?"

I don't know about you, but I don't want to be so broadminded that I don't stand for anything. I don't want my moral vision to become so blurred that I begin to call the darkness, light and the light, darkness.

My feelings echo the sentiments of a graduate student who made this plea in a letter to his pastor: "What am I asking? I want to hear someone who has the courage to say something besides 'anything goes.' I want to hear somebody say that virtue and morality are important. People I see sell out to the best sellers. Certain of my friends have ended up going down paths they didn't really want deep inside. They have discovered now the law of diminishing returns. One said to me, 'Really, after a while you don't feel guilty or uneasy about much of anything.' What are we to say to that? The loudest voices are being heard, and they are all saying, 'Do it. Do whatever you want. If you want to do it, it is right.' But it isn't right... it can't be!"

I believe that people all around us are crying out for us to stand up and be counted. They want to know that we believe there still is such a thing as right and wrong in the eyes of God. If we accept the idea that people can be responsible, then we must also accept the fact that some patterns of behavior are irresponsible and unacceptable.

Jesus' love for the adulterous woman did not prevent Him from calling her actions sinful. Indeed, His love for her required that He do precisely that. Anything less would not have been loving. Anything less would have indicated that she didn't count, that what she did with her life didn't matter. Don't you see, such broadmindedness is not love... such acceptance of unacceptable behavior is not love. It is the very antithesis of love. Because Jesus loved her, He said, "You have sinned."

II.

It's true, as I have said, that we must make moral judgments. Otherwise, life has no meaning. But we must make moral judgments without being judgmental. That's the second thing we must see in our scripture. And that's why Jesus had some words for those self-righteous people with rocks in their hands, preparing to pound the life from her body as penalty for her sin.

Please hear what I say now with your ears wide open, because it's essential to the issue at hand. As Christians we are to make moral distinctions, but never from the position of self-righteousness. We may identify someone's behavior as unacceptable or as sinful, but we must never assume, therefore, that we are better than they. The sinful behavior we see in another person may not be our particular problem, but we have sins of our own which will do just fine to keep us from any moral superiority.

The fact is that "all have sinned and have fallen short of the glory of God." The word is "all" and I presume that includes you and me. Jesus never glossed over the adulterous woman's behavior. He never excused it. He never approved of it. But He did say to the mob that they were not to punish her unless they could claim sinless perfection.

No human being can claim such perfection. Each of us is in need of the love and forgiveness of God. Our relative moral superiority or inferiority begins to pale into insignificance when seen in the light of our common need for God's mercy. So, we are never to feel better than, or superior to, any other human being. We are to make moral judgments, but not to become proud and judgmental.

That's a difficult balance to maintain. How unloving, how ungracious we Christians can be in the name of moral standards. I am thinking at this moment of a man who has impeccable moral standards. His ethical behavior is above reproach. But he uses his code of ethics as a club with which to punish people. He is so unloving and so ungracious in his morality. I like the prayer of a child who prayed, "O God, make the bad people good and the good people nice." A lot of us "good" people could be so much nicer! What we are looking for is morality without stuffiness, goodness without arrogance.

155

Look at the contrast between the mob and Jesus on that day. Jesus was uncompromising in His standards. But He applied them lovingly in an effort to bring new life. The mob also had high standards, at least as far as sexual morality was concerned, but they applied their standards self-righteously and brutally in an effort to destroy life. We are to have convictions, yes! Strong convictions. But those convictions are to be applied always with compassion, with the intent of bringing new life to every situation.

One further thing at this point. We are to make moral judgments according to the best that we know at this moment. And we are to act accordingly. But we must never assume that we have the final word, that we have all the truth. We must keep open minds and sensitive spirits, so that God can show us new truth.

I like Martin Luther's approach. You remember that in the sixteenth century he was speaking out against abuses in the church. He was asked to recant, to retract his accusations under threat of severe punishment. This was his reply: "Unless I am convinced by scripture or plain reason that I am wrong, I neither can nor will recant. It is not advisable or safe to go against one's conscience. Here I stand. I cannot do otherwise. May God help me."

He stood firmly for what he believed. He acted on his convictions, even at great cost. But he was willing to listen. He was willing to be persuaded... but not by popular vote... not by the pressure of prevailing culture... only by scripture or by plain reason. That's not bad criteria for us either.

III.

One final thing must be said. We are to have moral convictions... convictions of the highest moral standards. We

156

are to apply those standards to ourselves and to those around us, although they are not to be applied self-righteously or close-mindedly. But, and this is the final thing I want to say, if our high standards are violated... if sins are committed, we are never justified in cutting the offenders off from our love and our concern. The proper Christian response is not condemnation but forgiveness!

That's the moral tightrope we Christians are called upon to walk. We are to make no compromise with the highest moral standards. We are to ask for and expect high levels of ethical behavior from ourselves and others. We are to ask for that and expect that precisely because we are loving people and precisely because we care what happens to people. And surely we understand by now that Christ makes moral demands upon us not in order to inhibit us, but because that's the direction in which life is to be found. He wants to give us the fullest possible experience of life... that's why He asks so much of us. So, I repeat, we must not make any compromise with the highest standards.

At the same time, we must never make our love conditional upon a person's behavior. A person is of infinite worth in the eyes of God no matter how he acts. So, when a person fails to live up to the highest standards... when a person sins, we are to reach out to him in love and extend to him the offer of forgiveness.

How we respond to such a person in such a situation will reveal the extent to which we are recipients of such gifts from God. If we have been loved, then we are to love. If we have been forgiven, then we are to forgive. As followers of the Christ, we must never be caught saying, "I'll love you when... I'll love you if... I'll love you as along as." No, our love must be unconditional. Our proper response is to say, "I love you... I forgive you." Period. But that doesn't mean that I expect any less from you. The standards are still high.

Looking again at our scripture, we see that Jesus had no interest in punishing the sinful woman. The mob was calling for punishment, but not Jesus. Jesus was interested in helping the woman find new life.

He did that, not by pretending that she hadn't sinned... not by saying that behavior didn't matter... indeed, He told her to change her ways, not to continue her sinful behavior. But He let her know that His love for her was not contingent upon that. The change He asked for was not so much for Him as for her because in that direction was life.

The story is one of the most beautiful in scripture. Jesus confronted the angry mob, ready any moment to begin pounding the life from her body. He said, "He who is without sin among you, let him cast the first stone." One by one they dropped their stones and quietly walked away. Then He turned to the woman, no doubt shivering in fear, and said, "Where are your accusers? Has no one condemned you?" She looked around and said, "No one Lord." Jesus said, "Neither do I condemn you. Go, and sin no more."

There's no doubt about it. Christ has convictions about behavior. But those convictions are always applied with compassion, with love and forgiveness.

Let me say it like this: Years ago, at her annual Birthday Honors Party, Queen Elizabeth honored John Profumo. Do you remember him? He was the major figure in a scandal that rocked the British Empire. The press reported that Profumo was involved in an affair with a call girl from London, who in turn was involved with Russian spies. When this was brought to light, Profumo made the matter worse by lying to the

House of Commons. Later, he had a change of heart, went to the Prime Minister, confessed and resigned from the cabinet. Since that time he dropped from public notice. He quietly went to work in the slums of London, attempting to be of help to the lonely and lost. No doubt, for him, it was a kind of personal penance. Years later, at the Honors Party, Elizabeth, the Queen, named John Profumo, the sinner, among the distinguished citizens of her realm.

Isn't that great! Now note, Queen Elizabeth did not say that what he did was o.k. What she said was that what he did is forgiven!

That's our stance. We don't use high moral standards as a club, but as a call to fullness of life in Christ. And when a brother or sister stumbles, we don't accuse, we forgive and we extend a helping hand. As followers of the Christ, we must be people of conviction, but we must also be people with compassion.

Prayer: God, our Father, save us from moral indifference, from ethical wishy washiness, from behavioral blindness. Help us to insist upon the highest of standards from ourselves and from others precisely because we care about them. At the same time, Father, save us from self-righteousness and from close-mindedness. Give us the spirit of our Lord. Help us to reject sin, while accepting the sinner. Help us to love because we have been loved. Enable us to forgive because we have been forgiven. In the name of Christ we pray. Amen

.

Love's Not Love Unless...

John 3:16

It was one of those lazy Sunday afternoons. I was relaxing in the recliner in front of the TV set. One eye was watching, the other eye was sleeping. It was that time of day just made to order for turning on an old black and white movie and allowing it to help you doze.

I was all prepared for that. I had been up late the night before and could use the nap. But somehow the movie caught my attention and soon both eyes were awake and watching. The movie was "Roman Holiday" starring Gregory Peck and Audrey Hepburn. By today's standards the plot was simple, the characters not well developed, the dialogue simplistic, and the camera work unimaginative. But I liked it. (I suppose at heart I am a simple, romantic sort!)

In the movie, Audrey Hepburn was a British princess making a good will tour of Europe. She became tired of the responsibility, the regimentation, and the isolation of the royal life, so she decided to run away and have herself a holiday as a commoner. Rome was the city in which she escaped. And of course, predictably, she met Gregory Peck, an American journalist looking for a story. He agreed to show her the sights. And for twenty-four hours they shared all of the wonderful, romantic experiences which Rome affords.

Neither of them intended it, but they fell in love. They knew it was impossible, she was royalty, he was a commoner. They had no future together. But they could not deny their feelings. They were deeply, hopelessly in love, and it felt good. They were alive with the feelings of it. But she had a duty to her country and to her royal family, so after her twenty-four hour Roman holiday, she embraced her responsibility and returned to her family.

The concluding scene was a touching one. There was a press conference with newsmen from all over the world in attendance. The princess, exuding poise and royal dignity, looked out across the assemblage. Her eyes met his and just for a moment she lost her composure. It was obvious that all of those loving feelings came rushing back to both of them. But they could not speak and they could not acknowledge their relationship. That was a moment of real pain and I experienced something of it along with them.

They were in love, but they were not free to express their love. They were in love, but they repressed it and lived the rest of their lives without ever doing anything about it. Right then and there this chapter was given birth, because I saw something or I sensed something that I had not sensed before in quite that way.

I was pulling for them to break down the barriers and express their love. I wanted them to break their silence and proclaim it to the world. It just didn't seem right that they should feel so strongly and yet refuse to act out their feelings. And it came to me at that moment that, when it is real, love wants – love needs to be expressed.

162

I.

That is the first thing I want to say. It is the nature of love to demand expression. Love is never complete unless it is acted out, communicated, expressed.

That may come as close as anything to getting at why you and I were created to begin with. Probably the first verse of scripture we learned was "God is love." That is a good place to begin, because probably the word "love" comes closer than any other to expressing the essential nature of God. But, don't you see if God is love, and if love is not complete unless it is expressed, then that explains us. Love cannot long exist without an object. God, being love, wanted someone to whom He could express Himself, someone to whom He could give the gift of love, so He called us into being. And the entire religious history of the human race is the story of this divine love reaching out to people like us seeking to make itself known.

Loving and giving go together. And I think that is why our scripture is among the all-time favorites. "For God so loved the world that He gave..." That is the nature of love, to give. Across many centuries God patiently called to His people, He pleaded with them. He sent prophets and messengers, calling them to that life for which they were created. Finally, when all was in readiness—the scriptures express it as "In the fullness of time" – when everything was prepared, God expressed Himself in the flesh of His Son, Jesus, the Christ.

That was the love of God expressed in a way that people could see it, rub shoulders with it, be touched and changed by it. "For God so loved the world that He gave His Son..." It is true isn't it? Loving and giving go together. Love is not complete unless it is expressed.

If you have ever been in love you know exactly what I am talking about. There is this something inside — we call it love — that is bursting to get out. Somehow it has to be expressed. Somehow it has to make itself known to the one it loves. And how frustrating that is! No action seems impressive enough. But still there is this something inside that demands to be expressed. We sense, don't we, that our love is not really love unless we can somehow convey it to the one we love.

If we can apply human emotions to God, God must have felt something like that as He has sought to make His love known to us for so long. We Christians believe that Jesus was the best of all efforts to make God's love known to us. It is a great story and a great verse of scripture describes it: "For God so loved the world that He gave His Son."

We have been talking about God expressing His love, and about lovers expressing their love. It should go without saying that the same principle applies when we talk about Christian love. Love is more than an emotion. It is more than words. Love is something you do. The New Testament speaks of love in very practical, down to earth terms. It speaks of feeding the hungry, clothing the naked, visiting the sick and imprisoned, forgiving your enemies, helping your neighbors… and doing all of these things as expressions of love. Such actions are reflections of divine love. God loves us, then we pass it on by loving others. But the principle stands — love is not love unless it is expressed!

II.

That brings us to the second thing I want to say, and that is that not just any kind of expression is good enough. Love must be expressed in appropriate ways, and that means doing whatever is in the best interests of the one you love. Please understand that love does not require us to do what another person wants. It requires that we do what they need. Christian love at its best is strong, not weak. It is life-giving, not life-denying.

I don't know about you, but I am getting just a little bit tired of the popular stereotype of a Christian pushover — a soft-headed and soft-hearted person who can be manipulated into doing almost anything in the name of love.

Of course, in all honesty, I have to admit that a great many destructive, life-denying things are done every day in the name of Christian love. Where did we ever get the idea that to love someone was to give them whatever they want or ask for? Where did we ever get the idea that a Christian is a Caspar Milquetoast who is everyone's "yes" man? That's not what my Bible says.

My Bible says that to love someone, to really love someone is not always popular. It is not always well received. Sometimes the most loving thing is to say "no" to them. To love someone with a strong love, a life-giving love is to offer them not what they want, always, but what they need. Even if that means that they don't like us anymore. That may be the cost of real love. Authentic Christian love is often costly, painful, risky. There is no guarantee that we will be loved in return, at least by that person. I tell you, you have to be strong to love in a life-giving way.

We parents are usually pretty careful to provide good nutrition for our children. We wouldn't think of feeding our children cotton candy and popsicles for breakfast, ice cream sundaes for lunch, and candy bars and pop for dinner. We wouldn't do that even if they begged us. But I see people providing that kind of emotional diet every day. In the name of love they accommodate, they protect, they indulge, they make weak and dependent.

I have been far more guilty of that than I like to admit. But do you know what I have discovered lately? In the name of love I have done so many things that people have wanted or asked for. Even when they were not in the best interests of the other person. I have done them, claiming that my action is an expression of my love for them. But that is not so. In reality, my action is an attempt to get them to love me.

Do you see the distinction? When I am trying to get someone to love me, I will do whatever I think will please them, even when it is not in their best interests. But when I love wisely and strongly, I will do what is in their best interests even when they hate me for it. Do you understand what I mean, then, when I say that love must be expressed in appropriate ways?

That is the way God has loved us throughout history. Time and again God has refused to give us what we wanted. He keeps insisting upon giving us what we need. Nobody wanted Jesus, but God sent Him as the supreme expression of His love. And when Jesus began His public ministry, He refused to tailor it to the desires of the people. Don't you see, Jesus would never have been crucified if He had given the people what they wanted, but his love was stronger than that. He gave them what they needed and they killed Him for it.

We have been saved because God refuses to indulge us, to spoil us, to cater to us. That is why I resent so strongly some contemporary preachers who distort the Christian faith. They turn a strong, rugged, life-giving faith into a cotton candy sentimentality, too weak to give us more than illusion and transient security. They present God as a celestial grandfather who exists for the purpose of running our

166

errands, seconding our motions, and giving us everything we want and little of what we need.

That is not the God of the New Testament! That God gives us not what we want, but what we need. And He keeps on offering it to us even when we say "no," even when we turn our backs and go off in other directions. But if we ever see the meaning of His gift and reach out in faith to take hold of it... let's let our scripture say it: "For God so loved the world that He gave His only Son, that whoever believes in Him shall not perish, but have everlasting life."

God's love for us is our model for loving. So, in all of our relationships – home, school, work, friends – we are to love with strength and wisdom. We are to reach out to others with the best interests in mind. We are to help meet their needs, no matter how they feel about us in return. Our love is to be a gift, no strings attached.

Let me say it again. Love is not complete unless it is expressed. But it must be expressed in appropriate, life-giving ways.

III.

The third and final thing I want to say is that when we give love away the result is that we have more than we started with. That is the remarkable thing about God's economy, and is a further evidence of His love for all of us. We are not rationed in our supply of love. We don't have to conserve it or hoard it. The remarkable thing about love is that it doesn't fit normal mathematical categories. There seems to be an abundant, even endless supply. Years ago, I read a magazine article which was an interview with Steve Allen, the entertainer. Steve said some things which have stayed with me through the passage of time. He told of how he and his wife, Jayne Meadows had adopted a child. They gave that child all the love they had to give. Then they adopted a second child and a third. They loved those two children equally as much as they loved the first. The amazing thing was that they could give love to a number of children without having to reduce in any way their love for the first. The article contained some poetry written by Steve Allen. I can't quote it, but I have never forgotten the central idea: "Love is infinitely divisible!" You can keep adding to the list of those you love without having to reduce your love for those who were the first. And, as a bonus, the more love we give away, the more we seem to have!

That is the way God made the world. According to His design, the more love we give, the more we receive. The more we give away, the more we have. So many people sit around waiting to get. They have never learned that happiness is in giving. That is the way it is, because that is the way God made it to be. As St. Francis of Assisi said in his great prayer, "It is in giving that we receive."

Richard Lessor has written a delightful little children's book called, "Fuzzies" which says it. There was once a beautiful little isolated valley in which all the people were happy all of the time. And, in large measure, they were happy because they had "fuzzies." Fuzzies were like a little puff of soft fur – perfectly round, warm and soft. The little creatures were so soft and cuddly and looked up at you with such absolute trust as they curled up in your hand, that they made everybody happy.

In fact, just holding a fuzzy made you feel better. Over a period of years, the tradition of exchanging fuzzies came into being. People would carry the little creatures in "fuzzy bags" and give them to anyone they met. People were constantly exchanging fuzzies. Every time a person got a fuzzy it made him happy. The happier they got the more they wanted everyone else to be happy, so the more fuzzies they gave away. Everyone was happy, giving and receiving fuzzies until the wicked witch surveyed the scene. She was in charge of spreading the blahs and there were no blahs to be found in the happy valley. "This will never do," she said. And she decided upon a plan. She went into the valley and began to spread the rumor that there was to be a shortage of fuzzies, and that if you gave your fuzzies away, others may not give any to you and soon you would be completely out of fuzzies. Fear set in. People stopped giving fuzzies away. They began to hoard them and even lock them up in their attics or basements. But the little creatures could not live in such unhealthy environs and so gradually the fuzzies disappeared.

A freeway was built in the peaceful valley. They became a part of the outside world. The blahs set in, and they became just like everyone else. But one day a grandmother was telling the children about the old times in the valley and about how happy everyone had been when there were fuzzies around. And she asked herself, "I wonder what life would have been like if there hadn't been a shortage of fuzzies?"

Of course, you and I know that Richard Lessor was not really writing about fuzzies. He was writing about love. And although his story is fiction, what he says is true. When you worry about how much love you are getting… when you try to ration or withhold the love you give, the blahs set in and there is no happiness. But when you give love as if there is an endless supply, there is always more than enough to go around, and there is happiness everywhere.

Aren't those same dynamics present in Jesus' statement: "He who seeks to save his live – hold on to it, protect it, hoard it, save it – will lose it. But he who loses his life – uses it, gives it, shares it, invests it – will find it."

169

That is the new math, Christian style. Give and you will have!

For several years the Junior High UMYF at Church of the Good Shepherd in Arcadia, California, where our children grew up, closed their meetings by singing a delightful little song expressing the same idea. It was about a "Magic Penny," and the words were:

> "Love is something if you give it away, you end up
>   having more;
> It's just like a magic penny, hold it tight and you
>   won't have any;
> Lend it, spend it and you'll have so many they'll roll
>   all over the floor, so
> Love is something if you give it away, you end up
>   having more."

I believe that is one of God's greatest gifts to us. Isn't it great to live in the kind of world that the more you give away, the more you have!

Of course, the place where it all starts is with an experience of God's love. "For God so loved the world that He gave His only Son." That is the nature of love, to express itself. Once we receive that love from God, we pass it on to others: "We love because He first loved us." And the more of that love we give away to one another, the more we have and the more blessed life becomes. I think that's good news!

Prayer: Father, we are grateful for Your life-giving gift of love which comes to us in Christ. Help us to receive Your gift in faith and then to share it with all we meet. Let us not be afraid to love. Let us not be afraid to love strongly, wisely. Help us to love one another freely, extravagantly. We trust that it is in giving that we will receive. Hear our prayer as we make it in the name of Christ, your gift of love to us. Amen.

The Leap of Faith

Mark 9:14-29

There are a number of affirmations which are central to the Christian religion. We declare that God is a loving and powerful Father... that God has revealed Himself in Jesus, the Christ... that through Christ, God has redeemed the world and invited us all to be His sons and daughters. We affirm that we can make contact with God through prayer... that the more we come to experience God's love, the more we understand that we are brothers and sisters to all humanity, and that we are to relate to them in love and understanding, and we are to act with unconditional goodwill and with unselfish helpfulness. I could go on and on listing those realities which Christians have always declared to be important. But my guess is that you are as familiar with them as I am, so we don't need a re-statement of them now.

What we do need to understand is that every Christian affirmation is meaningless and irrelevant until it makes vital contact with your life or mine. All of the pretty ideas we think about, all of the hopeful words we say have nothing to do with anything until they take hold of us and become personal. There is nothing in all the world so pointless and empty as the concept of "God" until He becomes *my* God.

Now, the way all of this happens, we believe is through faith. Concepts become experiences through faith. Affirmations become realities through faith. The God "out there," thought about, talked about wished for, becomes the God "in here" encountered, experienced, trusted through faith. So, rightly understood, faith becomes the keystone by which Christian theory becomes Christian experience.

I.

Perhaps the place to begin is by talking about what faith is and is not. It is a badly misunderstood word. Most people think of faith as believing in something in the sense of giving intellectual agreement to an idea. Well, certainly faith involves belief, but belief alone can be irrelevant. For example, I might say, "I believe that there are little green men on Mars." I might intellectually agree with that idea, but that alone would have nothing to do with me. Whether or not that idea is true is a matter of indifference to me, because it does not affect the way I choose to live my life. Similarly, a great many people say, "I believe in God." And what they mean by that is that they give intellectual assent to the idea of God. But such a belief is irrelevant unless it affects the way we choose to live.

Now, faith in God does require belief in God. But it goes well beyond belief. Now hear this: faith means reliance. It means trust. Faith means the willingness to live your life as if something is so. Let me say it like this: I believe in the existence of airplanes. I believe that I could board a plane and fly from here to there in a short period of time. But such belief is not faith. And it is meaningless and irrelevant for me as long as I am content to merely talk about airplanes. It doesn't become faith until I actually board a plane, trust it with my life. And allow it to transport me from here to there.

That is faith. It is trusting in something... depending upon something... living your life on the basis of something.

So, it becomes obvious that if that is what faith is all about, every person lives by faith. You cannot live your life for even one day without faith. Today you are trusting something. You are depending upon something. You are living your life as if something is ultimately real, ultimately powerful, ultimately life-giving. Even the person who claims to be an atheist or an agnostic still lives his life as if something is more important than anything else. It may not be a conscious thing, but the fact is, we cannot live without faith... that is, we cannot live without relying upon something, depending upon something. As someone has said, "you can fail to make up your mind, but you cannot fail to make up your life."

Now here is the point: whatever you depend upon... whatever you rely upon... whatever you trust to be more real, more powerful, more life-giving than anything else... whatever that is for you, that is your God. No matter what you say, the thing upon which you build the foundation of your life is your God. So you see, it is quite possible to believe in the God who was revealed in Christ, but have that belief be quite irrelevant, because in fact your faith is in something else. You depend upon, you rely upon something else.

One of the saddest things I can imagine is for a person to live his entire life and die without ever consciously knowing who or what his god really is. It is possible to go through all of the motions of religion, profess and belief in all the creeds, think of ourselves as good, Church-going Christians, and yet all the while live our lives on the basis of some other center of meaning... in fact living our lives as if God doesn't exist!

In the gospels, Jesus kept reminding people that such a life just doesn't work out very well. Jesus said that only God is worthy of our faith. Nothing else will satisfy us. Nothing else will do what we need. He said that when we try to build on any other foundation, it is like building on sand. Sooner or later the entire structure will crumble.

Our Christian affirmation is that God is God. Rely upon Him. Depend upon Him. That is the only way that works. Live your life as if God is and as if He is like Jesus, because God can be trusted with your life. That is what faith is — reliance, trusting, living your life as if...

II.

Now I would like for us to think for a few moments about why faith in God is important. Assuming that every person has some sort of faith, what motivates us to reach out for Christian faith?

Let me say at the outset that motivation is important. You must want faith. Usually it does not come if it is a matter of indifference. Faith must be reached for, struggled with, grown into.

There is an old fable about a youth who sought out a sage and asked how he could obtain faith. The old man took the youth to a nearby stream, grabbed him by the neck, and plunged his head beneath the water. He held him there for what seemed like an eternity, the youth struggling and kicking to free himself. Finally he released him and the young man drew his head back gasping for breath. "What were you trying to do?" he said. "I almost drowned!" The wise man asked, "When you were under water, what did you want most?" "Air," he said immediately. Then the sage smiled and replied,

176

"When you want faith as much as you just wanted air, you will find it." Motivation is important.

Part of what motivates us to seek faith in God is our discovery that a great many things in life don't work very well. We may have taken some of God's greatest gifts to us and distorted them by trying to make them into gods. We have tried to make them carry the full weight of our lives. We have depended upon them to give us meaning or to make us happy, always with less than satisfactory results. Perhaps we have trusted in our jobs, our reputations, money, our spouses, our children, or some other center of value... all good gifts of God. But none is capable of carrying the full weight of our lives. None can make us feel like meaningful, significant persons. None can provide the sense of self-worth for which we all long. God is God! And nothing is going to work out until we acknowledge that and center our lives around Him. That is faith.

As I look around me, I see so many people trying this and then that. They are looking for something that is trustworthy, dependable... something strong enough to build upon. But they keep being hurt and disappointed because the things they depend upon keep failing them. You know, there are so many shiny, glittering things in the world that promise so much and deliver so little. But the bottom line is always exactly when Augustine said it was. "Thou hast made us for Thyself, O God, and our hearts are restless 'til they find their rest in Thee." There is that God-shaped empty place in the center of our lives. We may try for years to fill that void with a variety of other shapes, but only God can do what we need. That is part of our motivation to seek faith in God. We have tried so many other things that haven't worked.

A second part of our motivation is that in the midst of our search for a life-style that works , we may encounter someone who has faith and whose life is so attractive and so contagious. I believe that God reaches out to us through other people. And I believe that every person of faith "caught" his faith from some other person or group of persons. We see in that person's life something that is real, something that is authentic. When we are with them, we feel alive! We look at them and we say to ourselves, "Whatever it is they've got, I want it." So, on the basis of that contagious contact, we reach out for faith. That may be the most prevalent motivation of all – we are all reaching out for a life that works.

III.

There is one more thing I want to talk about. If we understand what faith is, and if we decide we want it, how do we get it? That is the question.

The first suggestion I make is that if you are serious about wanting an authentic, life-giving Christian faith, you must go where faith is. You will never develop a faith if you spend most of your time with faithless people. Faith does not emerge from a vacuum. It is contagious. You get it from people who have it. That is one reason the Church is important. We are a community built on faith. We gather as a church either because we have faith or because we are searching for it. That is what we are about. It is in the community of God's people that faith is nurtured and strengthened. That is the first suggestion: regularly, systematically go where faith is.

The second suggestion is to practice what the Church has called "holy habits," or the "means of grace." I am talking about worship, the reading of the Bible, prayer, the sacraments. For twenty centuries Christians have discovered that through such disciplines they could place themselves in the channel of God's grace. Such holy habits are the means by which we open ourselves up and allow God to work within us. So that is the second suggestion: practice the holy habits.

The third suggestion is perhaps the most important of all. If you would have faith, begin to live now as if you do have faith. That may be one of the most important things you will ever hear about the Christian faith, so let me say it again: If you would have faith, begin to live now as if you do have faith.

Most people I know get things backwards. They say, "Prove the Christian faith to me and then I will believe it." For years I tried to meet their request. I tried to persuade, to argue, to prove, but it cannot be done. So, you might as well accept it here and now: there is no way to prove the existence of God. Whatever is ultimately real, ultimately true, ultimately powerful must be a matter of faith, not proof. So our dealing with God is always a matter of faith. It involves taking a risk... sticking our necks out. It involves the willingness to live our lives as if there is a God before we know of a certainty that there is. As someone has said, "Faith is betting your life that there is a God."

The only proof of the Christian faith is experiential proof. There is a sense in which the Christian faith cannot be understood except from the inside. You can't have it proven to you before you try it. You must try it and in so doing it is proven in your own experience. The proof is experiential.

You know there are some things in life which simply cannot be understood apart from the experience of them. Try to learn about love from a textbook, for example. Try to prove the existence of love to someone who has never been in love and you will discover what I mean. "Loving" has

179

meaning for us only when we have experienced the reality of loving.

Let me say it like this. Walt Disney made a film some years ago about the American eagle. The film shows how eagles go high upon the cliff to build their nests and raise their young. It is a very moving experience to see the little eagle look out of the nest into the great chasm where he is going to have to learn to fly. There is no way for him to be sure in advance that he can fly. There is no way for him to know what flying is like until he tries it. What he does know is that it is not much fun to stay in the nest. He knows that other eagles are flying. So, with that much evidence to urge him on, the little eagle takes the leap of faith and discovers that he can fly!

I believe that faith in God is much like that. Perhaps you have never experienced spiritual goose bumps. Maybe, at the feeling level, you have never been aware of God. That is not unusual. But maybe you have discovered a lot of things in life that don't work. You have discovered some foundations that crumble under too much weight. Maybe you are searching and haven't found anything really satisfying.

At the same time, perhaps you have met a few people somewhere along the way who seem to have put it all together. There is a special something about them that is attractive. They seem to be getting more out of life and putting more into life than we are. And the thing that makes the difference for them, they say, is God.

How do we know that what they say is true? How do we know that Christian faith is not just a fairy tale? How do we know that God is not just wishful thinking? How do we know? The only honest answer is that we don't. And the only way to find out is to risk the leap of faith.

What I mean by that is that we decide to live by faith in God. We will live as if what the Christian faith says about God is true. We will live as God would want us to live if He existed. I don't know of any other way to do it. You have got to live as if the Christian faith is true before you can know whether or or not it is true. It is only after you have taken the risk... only after you have experienced it for yourself that you can then say, "I know!"

Do you remember the father mentioned in our scripture. He wanted his son to be cured. He wasn't sure how much he believed in Jesus. But his son had been sick since his birth. And he had tried everything else he had known to try. Jesus came along and with Him came stories of people who had been healed. So the father reached out with limited faith and said, "If you can do anything, have pity on us and help us." Jesus said, (What do you mean) "If you can! All things are possible to him to believes." Then the father said, "Lord, I believe. Help my unbelief."

I think that is one of the great passages of scripture. The father did not wait until he was a giant of faith. He acted on what faith he had, at the same time praying for more. And that is exactly the way it works. If you don't have any faith, you act "as if." If you have a little faith, you use what you have. But it is by acting by faith that faith grows.

Look at the example of the disciples. When they were called into discipleship by Jesus they didn't know who He was or where He was taking them. It was a risky thing to leave their families and secure pattern of living and follow Him. They had to take a leap of faith. But don't you see, they had to follow Him before they could learn who He was. First they acted on faith, then they felt the faith.

It is true: living the faith is the only way to know the faith. First you act, "as if..." then you come to know. Robert Goodrich wrote about a college student who was struggling with his faith.. Christianity was difficult for him because God had never been real in his experience, But one Christmas he used his holidays to get a job in the post office. With the money he earned he purchased food and gifts for a family where the father was out of work and there had been a great deal of illness. He delivered his basket personally on Christmas eve. And afterward he said that it was when he looked into the faces of that family that God became real for him. As he put it. "As I came down the steps from that door, I felt God's presence: He was real for me."

Do you hear it? It was by doing that he began to feel. It was by acting "as if..." that he came to know!

In the final analysis that is the only way to know. We know the Christian faith is true only when we have experienced the truth of it in our lives.

The closing paragraph of Albert Schweitzer's book, "The Quest of the Historical Jesus" says it. Will you hear these words as catching up the essence of what I have tried to say?

> "He comes to us as one unknown, without a name, as of old, by the lakeside He came to those men who knew Him not He speaks to us the same word: 'Follow thou me! And sets us to the tasks which He has to fulfill for our time. He commands. And to those who obey him, whether they be wise or simple, He will reveal himself in the toils, the conflicts, the sufferings which they shall pass through in his fellowship. And, as an ineffable mystery, they shall learn in their own experience who He is."

I dare you to take the leap of faith. Begin now to live as if.. "Lord, I believe. Help my unbelief."

Prayer: Loving God, our Father, help us now to take the leap of faith. Help us to begin in this moment to live as if You are God and as if You are calling us to follow Your Son Jesus, the Christ. And grant, Father, that as we live as if these things are true, we will discover the truth of them in our experience. In the name of Christ we pray. Amen.

When Trouble Comes

Matthew 27:45-46; Matthew 28:20

I remember seeing a cartoon in a magazine depicting a young man in trouble. He was hanging by his fingertips to the edge of a precipice. Some distance below, there was an alligator with his eyes fixed on the young man, his jaws open wide in anticipation of his next meal. And, if that were not enough, from above there was a boulder that had been dislodged, and it was falling in the direction of this young man's head. The caption beneath the picture said, "When things seem like they can't possibly get any worse, they usually do."

We all have days when we feel like that, don't we? Troubles come to us, troubles so large or so numerous or so perplexing that we wonder whether or not we can survive them. And, sad to say, such experiences are not the exception in life, they are the rule. If you haven't had trouble yet, just wait, because to be a human being in this world is to experience trouble that demands a response. The time will come for us all when we will echo Jesus' words from the cross, "My God, my God, why!"

Some tragedies are more easily understood than others. I can understand trouble which is the result of human choices. I don't like that kind of trouble any better, but I can

185

understand it. A person goes out and drinks too much, gets in his car and tries to drive home. The driver fails to see a stop sign, hits another car, and innocent people are killed. Or, a man comes home and says to his wife, "I don't love you any more. I want a divorce." It's not what she wants, not what the children want, but people are hurt because of the choice that someone makes. Both of those situations involve choice. When God created us and gave us the gift of freedom, that gift carried with it the possibility of people using their freedom to do harm as well as to do good. So, the choices people make result in much of the trouble we encounter every day. Whether those choices are deliberate, or ignorant, or simply irresponsible and careless, the wrong choices can hurt. As I have said, I can understand that kind of trouble. I don't like it, it doesn't hurt any less just because I can understand it, but I can at least understand that kind of trouble.

But trouble that comes through no apparent human choice is what gives me sleepless nights: tsunamis, hurricanes, tornadoes, crib death, cancer, death in child birth, tragedies like those. Even when an explanation is attempted, it is less than satisfactory. At one level I can understand a shift in the earth's crust, displacing tons of water, creating a tidal wave, resulting in death and destruction. My mind can process those facts. A blood vessel hemorrhages, the doctors can't stop the bleeding, and the result is shock and death. The physical laws, which usually work for our good, can sometimes work to create hurt and heartbreak. I can understand that, but even if I understand that at some level, I still will ask, "Why is the world structured in such a way as to allow for that?"

And, the very thing that adds such meaning to life, the ability to love one another, is also the thing that enlarges the likelihood of hurt. Our love makes us vulnerable. Even when trouble does not come to us directly, when it comes to someone we love, we are drawn into the hurt of it. We suffer along with our loved one precisely because of our love. If we did not love so much, we could not be so easily hurt, but it is our capacity for loving that that makes life worth living. So, that experience that is at the heart of life's meaning sets us up for hurt when trouble comes.

And even understanding the reason for such hurt does not help very much. If it were my wife, my children, or my grandchildren killed by that drunken driver, to understand that the driver was impaired, and that the laws of physics and physiology which usually work for our good caused their death in that instance, that understanding does not help. It just doesn't!

Too many times in my life I have stood with victims of such heartbreak, shaken my fist at heaven, and said, "My God, my God, why?" Understand that when we say such a thing, we are not asking for an explanation. An explanation won't help very much. What we are saying is, "I protest. I don't like it like this. I don't like the reality of living in a world in which such tragedies occur. I protest!"

It helps to know that Jesus experienced it too. At the cross, forsaken by his friends, betrayed by his enemies, exhausted and in pain, Jesus felt alone and desolate. He too cried out, "My God, my God, why have you forsaken me?" It helps to realize that Jesus knows, He understands. He's been there. And, it helps to believe, as I do, that God never intends for hurtful things to happen to his children. Because of human freedom and natural law, God allows it, but He never intends it. God loves us and wants only good things for us. Do any of us parents and grandparents want anything hurtful to happen to those we love? Of course not! Jesus said, "If you, being evil (not really evil, but in comparison to God's goodness...) – if you, being evil, know how to give good gifts to your children, how much more will your Father in heaven give good things to those who ask him!" (Matthew 7:11) The God I have come to know in Jesus never wants bad things to happen to his children. In fact, I'll take it one step further: I believe that when we suffer, God suffers along with us. When we are in tears, God weeps with us. God's love for us makes Him vulnerable too, just as our love for our families and friends makes us vulnerable to suffering. Somehow it helps, knowing that God is with us in all the troubles of life and that God shares our sorrow.

Jesus believed that. Even while upon the cross, even while saying, "My God, my God, why?" Jesus was directing those words to God. It was a prayer, actually quoting the beginning of Psalms 22. He was too exhausted to finish it, but we can. Just see what that Psalm says. After it says, "My God, my God, why have you forsaken me?" it goes on to say, confidently, "In you our ancestors trusted; they trusted and you delivered them. To you they cried, and were saved; in you they trusted, and were not put to shame." Jesus was not saying He believed that God would deliver Him from death. He was saying that even in the presence of death, He still put his trust in God, He still believed that God's grace and strength would sustain Him then as they had throughout his life.

I like to remember that most troubles, however disappointing and painful, are fleeting. I remember what an old country preacher said. Asked by a member of his congregation about his favorite Bible verse, he replied, "My favorite Bible verse is, 'And it came to pass.' The tough times of life don't come to stay. They come to pass." It's true that most troubles don't stay, but while they are here, they are difficult to manage.

The question is, what are we to do when troubles come our way. Are there resources we can draw upon? Troubles always present us with a crisis. The Chinese word for crisis involves two characters which symbolize danger and opportunity. So, a crisis is a dangerous opportunity. The danger is our inclination to give up. The danger is our inclination to isolate ourselves from others, and to become bitter and resentful. Such reactions are understandable, but they do not take us anywhere good. It is of pivotal importance what we do when trouble comes. Do you remember the poem,

> "One ship sails East, and another West,
> By the self-same winds that blow;
> 'Tis the set of the sails and not the gales
> That tells the way we go."

We all know people whose sails are set to catch the winds of bitterness and despair. They allow their trouble to destroy their lives. At the same time, we know people whose sails are set to catch the winds of God. They catch the winds of love and good will of caring people. They not only endure their trouble, they allow it to take them in a good new direction. The same external situation, but some are destroyed and others survive and even prosper!

So, what are we to do when trouble comes? To begin with, we must be determined to survive. At the outset, our pain may be such that that is the best we can do. We just endure. We put one foot in front of the other and get from one day to the next. One of the most beautiful prayers I ever heard consists of just four words: "Thank God for sunsets." That's a prayer of gratitude for the fact that we can break up the troubles of life and handle them one day at a time. Jesus said, "Do not worry about tomorrow, for tomorrow will bring worries of its own. Today's trouble is enough for today." (Matthew 6:34) If we isolate our troubles and deal with them one day at a time, determined just to get through today, we may be surprised at how manageable many of our troubles turn out to be.

And, while we are weak and in that moment have little hope for the future, we can allow our friends and loved ones to sustain us. I don't know why we are inclined to withdraw into ourselves and cut ourselves off from others precisely at those times when we need others the most. There is nothing courageous or noble about bearing our troubles alone. God never intended that. The longer I live, the more convinced I become that we were created to live not in isolation, but in relationship, loving, trusting, and supporting relationship. Everyone needs someone with whom we can share our feelings, our fears, and our hurts, someone with whom we can let down our defenses and be real. Perhaps this friend won't have all the answers. Maybe the friend won't have *any* answers. But if our friend can listen, understand, and care, then such a relationship can help us immeasurably. We can ride "piggy back" on the love and strength of those around us until we begin to gain some strength of our own. I have often said and written that in loving relationships our joys are doubled and our sorrows are cut in half. That is the way God does math. There is something about isolation that makes any trouble loom larger. At the same time, there is something about togetherness that makes any difficulty more bearable. I have come to believe that we can handle anything as long as we don't have to face it alone. With loving friends and family, we can make it!

Second, remember the difficult times you have already endured. Trust that all the dynamics that helped you get through the last difficulty are available to you still. I can't tell you how many times in my life I have found myself singing, "Through many dangers, toils and snares I have already

190

come; 'tis grace has brought me safe thus far, and grace will lead me home."

Finally, trust that you are not alone. God is with you, and his love and strength will see you through. Jesus believed that. Even though at the cross He felt alone and abandoned, He called upon God in prayer. He trusted that God was there. That trust was so important to Him then, that after the resurrection, the last thing Jesus said to his disciples and to us was, "Remember, I am with you always, even to the end of the world." God, we need that! There are times of trouble in life when our best efforts are not enough. Our wisdom is not wise enough and our strength is not strong enough. There are times when nothing will do what we need except God's grace and strength.

I know that at the onslaught of serious trouble we may not feel the truth of that. We may be in so much pain and desolation that we cannot see anything clearly or sense any hope anywhere. God understands that and feels the sorrow of that along with us. But listen now, I'm about to say something important: faith is not the same as feelings! You don't have to have goose bumps down the spine in order to act on faith. Faith is not feelings, faith is trust. It is an act of the will. Faith is trusting God, even when you *feel* that God is nowhere to be found. Faith is trusting that God is with us and that his grace and strength are sufficient to help us through, even when our feelings do not confirm that.

That is what Jesus did. At the cross He *felt* abandoned and all alone. His pain and sorrow overwhelmed him. Can you get in touch with the feelings of that? And yet...and yet, He trusted in God. He prayed to God even though He felt abandoned by God. Do you understand? You can have faith, you can act on trust, even when your feelings are taking you in a different direction.

191

Let me share with you a favorite quote that has sustained me through some difficult times. It is one of those quotes that has lodged itself in my mind and heart and will not leave. I think God placed it there so firmly because He knows how much I need it. Listen: "Never doubt in the darkness what God has shown you in the light." Do you hear it? Remember those times when you *felt* God's presence. Remember those times when you were sure that God is here and that you are being held in God's strong and loving arms. That is the truth. That is the heart warming and life giving truth. So, in the time of trouble, you *trust* that, even if you don't *feel* that. You trust that Jesus keeps his promises, "Remember, I am with you always, even to the end of the world." You trust that. You hang on to that. You take strength and hope from that. "Never doubt in the darkness what God has shown you in the light."

One more thing: when you are in the throes of great trouble, probably you are not ready to hear this, but even though God does not intend disappointment and hurt for his children, there is absolutely nothing that can happen to us that God cannot use for good if we will allow it. As I look back upon my life, it is abundantly clear to me that the times of greatest struggle and pain were also the times of greatest personal growth. I didn't know it at the time – at the time my heart was breaking – but I know now that God was using my difficulty to produce a wiser, more sensitive, more loving Jim.

I like the way Thornton Wilder expressed it in his play, "The Angel That Troubled the Water." In the play, there is a man who stood at the healing pool of Bethesda, pleading with God to restore him to health. And angel came and whispered into his ear, "Stand back. Healing is not for you. Without your wound, where would your power be?" And then he said this significant thing, "In love's service, only the wounded soldiers can serve!" Don't ever forget that! When we have been wounded, God can then use us in his loving army to bring strength and comfort to others who are being wounded. This is not to say that God caused the difficulty so that He could use it – not that. But when, for whatever reason, the trouble came, God was able to use it for good. I now believe that there is nothing that can happen to us that God cannot use for good if we will allow it.

Think again about Jesus. When all the world had turned against Him and had Him crucified, it was an unspeakable tragedy. To take the best, the most loving human being the world had ever seen, and then to reject him, to abandon him, to ridicule him, to torture him, and to put Him to death, is a tragedy of cosmic proportions. But God took all of that, shaped it by his powerful hands, and turned it into a resurrection! That tragic Friday of crucifixion, you know what we call it today. We call it Good Friday. It is good not because of all that happened on that day, but because of what God did with it, and he's doing it still! Our God is in the business of bringing resurrections out of all the crucifying experiences of life! So, be open to that. Allow for that. Trust God for that, and it will come!

So, when trouble comes, hang on. Put forth your best efforts. Rely upon the love of family and friends, allowing yourself to be sustained by their strength. And, in spite of any feelings to the contrary, trust that God is with you, and that his grace and strength will see you through.

Let me tie it all together by a narrative. He was an old man, living on the ragged edge of poverty in a rundown house at the edge of town. He lived alone except for an old dog who had been his longtime, constant companion. His circumstances were impoverished, but his spirit was not. He was a man of deep faith. One night, he knelt beside his bed, one arm draped over his dog, and he prayed this prayer:

193

"Good Master, we've come a long way together. We've had a lot of experiences together, you and me. I don't know what's waiting for me out there tomorrow, but I know this: ain't nothing going to happen that you and me can't handle."

Isn't that great! "ain't nothing going to happen that you and me together can't handle." To know that and to trust that is to be able to cope when trouble comes.

Prayer: Loving Father, the troubles of life are too tough for us alone. Help us to recognize our weakness so that we may rely upon you and become strong. Give us your grace, and help us to trust in its sufficiency in every time of trouble. In Jesus' name we pray. Amen.

I Believe In The Church

Ephesians 2:19-20

Eighty-three years ago I was born into the family of a Methodist minister. I have been in worship every Sunday since before I can remember. My earliest thoughts were influenced by the Sunday School. I became a member of the Church when I was eight years old. And, although I did not fully understand my decision, it was a deeply meaningful experience, and I will never forget it. As I grew older, my life was shaped by M.Y.F. groups and Church camps. I was educated in Church-supported schools. In so many ways I have been loved and cared about by Church people. My closest friends have been found in the Church. The Church introduced me to Christ, and through Christ I have come to know God. Because of the Church, I have come to know something of who I am and what life is all about. At every stage of my life the Church has been there, supporting, guiding, strengthening, loving. The fact is, all that I am and all that I hope to become I owe to the Church. That is why I say openly and unapologetically, "I believe in the Church!"

I say that with my eyes wide open, fully aware of the fact that the Church is far from perfect. Of course, the Church could not be perfect as long as I am a part of it. There are days when I identify with the comment attributed to Groucho Marx: "I would not belong to a club that would have me as a member." It stands to reason that there will be weaknesses and shortcomings in the Church as long as people like us are permitted to be a part of it. But that is at least a part of the glory of the Church, and it is positive proof that God is at work in it. If God were not at the center of His Church, people like us would have killed it long ago!

And think about this: one reason we criticize the Church so severely is precisely because we measure it by the high standards given to us by the Church! It is true that the Church never measures up to her Lord. But we know that because that very Church introduced us to Christ and made us painfully aware of the gap between where we are and where we need to be if we are true to our highest nature.

The fact is, if we are Christians, we have no alternative to the Church. Christ and His Church are bound inseparably together. To be a Christian is to be a part of it. There is no substitute. No one else even attempts to do what we attempt to do as the church. No one else raises the questions we raise. No one else provides the meaning that we receive from that fellowship. No one else tempts us to become all that we can become. No one else can introduce us to the Christ whom we meet through the church. To be a Christian is to be a part of the Church!

The early Church used to say that God is our Father and the Church is our mother. That has been my experience, too. I was born in the Church's womb and nourished at her breast. That is why I say, "I believe in the Church!"

Now when I use that word, "Church," I am not talking about a building, although we do construct and use buildings. And I am not talking about an organization, although we are organized. I am talking about people – people who belong to one another because they belong to the same Father. The Church is people with the Spirit of God at work in their midst.

That is what Paul was getting at in our scripture. He was writing to the Gentile Christians, people who up to that time had not been included as members of the family of God. That was a privilege afforded only to the Jews, the chosen ones. But Paul says, "You are no longer strangers and sojourners…" You aren't slaves or second-class citizens or transients wandering through. Listen, you are members of the family of God, with all of the rights and privileges which come with that. You are part of the family! You belong! You are a part of the Church!

Perhaps that is a good place to begin this chapter. I want to say three things about what it means to be a part of the Church.

I.

The first thing I want to say is that when you are a part of the Church, that becomes your basic identity in life. Rightly understood, the Church is not a place where we go or an organization to which we belong. It is who we are. It is our basic identity.

Let me say it like this: My life has been touched and changed by God. I have experienced something of His love and forgiveness. Through Christ I have come to know who I am and I have come to understand life as God's good creation. I believe that the world belongs to God. God loves it. He has a purpose for it. And all of life works out best when we understand that purpose and cooperate with it. We in the Church share a common vision of who we are and what life is, and we are called by God to live out that vision in everything we do each day. The living out of that vision is what the church is all about.

We are not the Church just when we are together in worship. We are not the Church only when we are gathered. No, we are the Church wherever we are, whatever we are doing, because that is our basic identity. We are the Church at home, at work, at school, among our friends.

You ask me who I am and I will tell you that I am Jim McCormick. That is true, but that is not the whole truth and not the deepest truth about me. In reality, I am one of the people of God. I am a part of the Body of Christ. I am the Church, wherever I am and whatever I am doing.

When we gather for worship or for study, it is our way of reminding ourselves of who God is and who we are, and as a result, how we are to live our lives. Apart from this experience in the Christian fellowship we are in danger of forgetting, and when we do, nothing makes any sense anymore.

There is a two-fold motion to the Church. We gather and then we scatter. We gather for worship, for study, for nurture, for mission. Then we scatter. We go to our homes, our places of business, our community organizations, our social groups. And whether we are gathered or scattered, our identity remains. We are the Church! Someone has compared this two-fold motion with a football game. We huddle and then we run a play. Both experiences are necessary. You can't run effective plays if you never huddle. And huddling loses meaning if we never run plays. Similarly, we cannot live as faithful Christians in our day to day world unless we take seriously the gathered fellowship of Christ. We meet together with other Christians to recharge our batteries, to renew our strength. And in that gathered community of faith, we are reminded of who we are.

Perhaps you are familiar with the story of a French soldier who was found suffering from amnesia. When he was picked up at a railroad station, he looked at his questioners blankly and all he could say was, "I don't know who I am. I don't know who I am." His identification papers had been lost and his face was disfigured, so no one could place him. Finally, they decided to take him from village to village, hoping that something would "click." When he entered the third village, a sudden faint light of recognition came into his eyes. He walked down a side street, began to hurry through a little gate, and then up the stairs, and finally rushing into his father's arms. In his father's house he knew who he was and where he belonged!

When we gather with the family of God, we too know who we are and what we are to do. We are the Church, and that is our basic identity in life.

II.

The second thing I want to say is that when you are a part of the Church, you are a part of a caring community. One of the major problems of our time is the problem of loneliness, of isolation. So many people live their lives each day surrounded by people, but with the feeling that they are not touching or being touched in any meaningful way. They feel separated, isolated, uncared for. They function, they perform, they accomplish, but they don't relate beneath the surface level. They don't feel loved, and that's so sad!

In every congregation I have served we have liked to talk about being a Church family. That is not just rhetoric. Increasingly it is becoming a reality. We all belong to God. I don't know what I would do without members of the Church family who encourage me to grow, who understand and forgive when I fail, but who love me enough to call for the best within me. That kind of nurturing and strengthening is something everyone needs.

When the Church is at its best, there is a sensitivity which causes us to identify with one another and to share experiences with one another. One person's joy is everyone's joy. One person's sorrow is everyone's sorrow. And somehow by sharing the joy is enlarged and the sorrow becomes manageable.

There is a verse from "Blest be the tie" that says it:

"We share each other's woes, our mutual burdens bear,
And often for each other flows the sympathizing tear."

When we understand the Christian faith, we understand that every Christian is to be a minister to every other person. We miss the mark if we think that the clergy are to be providers of ministry and the laity consumers of it. That is not the New Testament vision at all. According to scripture, every Christian is a minister, and the primary function of the clergy is to train and equip the laity for faithful and effective ministry! Each of us has a ministry to perform – a ministry of caring. You know, I have talked about that all my life. I have said that when the Church is truly the Church all its members are busy ministering to one another.

A number of years ago, Bernice White told about an experience she had at Holman Church in Los Angeles. Her brother suddenly, and without warning, became blind. Of course it was an experience of shock and sorrow for the entire family. On Sunday they were at worship and Bernice saw her brother come into the service with a cane, trying to find his seat. She couldn't take it. She dissolved into tears and went rushing from the sanctuary. She went into the ladies lounge and immediately found herself joined by one of the women in the congregation. The woman took Bernice in her arms, held her close and they cried together for about ten minutes. Finally, wiping the tears from her eyes, the woman said, "Sister, tell me, what are we crying about?" I like that story. She didn't know what the problem was, but she did know that a member of the family was in sorrow, and that was enough.

I see it happening in churches everywhere, and it is so life-giving. Someone is in the hospital, and friends go to call. There is a death notice in the newsletter and the telephone rings. The voice on the phone says, "I just heard about your loss and I wanted to tell you how sorry I am." A person is crying in the chapel. A friend sits down, puts an arm around the shoulder and says, "I'm sorry you're hurting. I want you to know I care." A letter arrives in the mail saying, "You looked troubled the other day. I'm thinking about you and praying for you. If there is anything I can do to help, please call." One person walks up to another and gives affirmation by saying, "I see growth taking place in your life. It looks good, and I want you to know that I'm happy for you."

God is touching and changing lives through that kind of sensitivity. People are listening, hearing, sharing, caring. To be loved in such ways feels better than anything I know. One person who had experienced such caring wrote about it like this:

"Your life has touched my life and
In you I have seen Christ.
His love has grasped me because you have accepted me,
Because your great, good kindness encircled me.
You are a sign pointed to all that can be.
Because I saw you walk as an agent of God's love
I see new possibilities for my life.

Now, I can be a Christ, the instrument of God's love to those of His children I will meet today."

Isn't that beautiful? That is happening among us. People are taking seriously their ministry to one another. It means more than I can say to belong to a family, the family of God. When I am a part of the Church I am not alone. I belong. I am loved and cared about and ministered to. Do you hear the good news in that? We are a family! We are the Church!

III.

One final thing. It is true that when you are a part of the Church, that becomes your basic identity. When you are a part of the Church you belong to a caring community, a family. But now a third thing is also true: when you are a part of the Church, you are on a mission for God.

Now, this is not optional. Our Christian mission is not something tacked on to the periphery of life. For those who understand the faith, our mission becomes the central task in life. Please understand that mission is not only sending a few dollars to a foreign land. Everything we do is mission. The Church is mission. As someone has said, "The Church exists by mission as a fire exists by burning." So, to be on mission is not optional.

The approach taken by the Church of the Savior in Washington, D.C., can inform us. I visited that congregation and studied it forty years ago. It is impossible to join that congregation and simply be a name on the membership roll. No, if you become a member, you sign up for one of their mission groups. The only way to be a part is to be a *working* part. For them, membership is mission.

Look at it like this. Christ is the Lord of the Church. Our scripture says, "Christ Jesus (is) the cornerstone" of the Church. To use Paul's imagery, Christ is the head, we are the body. So, we are to follow the instructions of Christ in getting done in the world things He wants done. Mission.

Part of our mission involves telling the story about what God has done for us in Christ. Somehow that story has got to be communicated. If God's love has touched us and changed us... if that experience has been life-giving for us, then we are obligated... no, we are privileged to share it. Somehow we must let people know that "God was in Christ, reconciling the world to Himself." We have got to share the good news that "God so loved the world that He gave His only Son, that whoever believes in Him should not perish but have eternal life." That is the gospel and it has got to be shared!

Words must be used, however reluctant we are to use them. Christians must be willing to put in a good word for Jesus. We must do it in appropriate ways. We must find a method that helps rather than hurts. Our words must be expressions of genuine caring, and they must be real... but words must be used.

Perhaps we would be less reluctant to talk about our faith if we understood clearly that we are not to talk about our goodness, but about God's grace. The emphasis is not upon what we have done, but upon what God is doing. Every Christian is to be "one beggar telling another beggar where to get food." And words must be used in accomplishing that task.

However, words alone are not enough. Our words will not convince anyone of anything unless they are accompanied by authentic, loving deeds. I am convinced that our Christian mission entails sticking our necks out, taking risks in an effort to help people in need. If we are the Body of Christ, that is, if we in the Church are to be the physical presence of Christ in the world today, then we must act in the 20th century as Jesus acted in the first. And that means caring, giving, helping. It means so identifying with the rest of humanity, that their needs become our needs. Then we extend a loving, helping hand.

Read the New Testament and you will discover that Christian love is so very practical. To love is to give what the other person needs, and to give it in the name of Christ.

Let me say it like this: a large number of people had embarked on a cruise. They were far out at sea, midway in their journey, when a man fell overboard and was in the process of drowning. Frantically he cried out for help. The ship's engines were stopped and all the passengers and crew gathered at the rail nearest the drowning man. They represented a cross-section of our culture, and each had a distinctive way of offering help.

A moralist among the group shouted: "You should have learned to swim when you were a child! Here is a book of ten easy lessons on how to swim!"

A disciple of positive thinking called out: "You're not really drowning. Think dry!"

An institutional bureaucrat droned: "Hang on! We've called a committee meeting and we're going to dialogue on it. If the situation warrants it we'll refer it to the budget committee. If they approve, we'll appoint a task force to organize a helping thrust into the water!" But the man continued to drown.

A traditional revivalist sees the man flailing about in the water and says: "I see that hand, brother. Is there another"

Fortunately, there is also a realist at the rail – a Christian. He simply and without fanfare takes off his clothes, jumps in, and rescues the drowning man. He identified with him, risks himself and does whatever is necessary to extend a helping hand. That's the Church at its best, and that's our mission – to love and care and serve wherever we are needed in the name of Christ. And it is not optional. Jesus said, "By this all people know that you are my disciples if you have love one for another."

To be on such a mission should not seem strange to us. It is really the most natural thing in the world. To be on a loving, helping mission is a logical expression of who we are. We are God's people, so we do God's business. We have been loved by God, so we pass that love on to others in the form of practical, loving service. And remarkably, the more we give, the more we have. We experience increased joy and deepened meaning when we love in practical and effective ways. That is one of the gifts of God's love to us, that He has made the world in such a way that all our lives are enhanced when we reach out to one another in loving service.

And the good news in all of this is that we are not alone as we seek to do God's will. We are not dependent upon our own resources alone. This is God's Church. God is present in the midst of his Church and He takes our efforts, blesses them, and uses them to do far more than we ever dreamed before. Jesus said, "Wherever two or three are gathered together in My name, there am I in the midst of them" That is what makes us a Church. Christ is Here! He is the One working in and through us. And the remarkable good news is that when we extend our hands in love, they become Christ's hands, and all whom they touch are given new life!

205

As I said at the beginning, I was eight years old when I became a member of the Church. Since that day the Church has been at the center of my life, and I have never regretted that for a moment. It is true in my experience that God is my Father and the Church is my mother. Together they have given me the richest gifts of life. That's why I say, I believe in the Church!

Prayer: Thank you Father for the church and for the privilege of being a part of it. Help us to see the church as our basic identity in life. Help us to take Jesus, the Lord of the church, as our model and guide. Enable us to walk in his company and to love and serve as He did. In his name we pray. Amen.

What More Can He Give?

Colossians 1:15-20

For 2000 years, the vitality of the Christian Church has been determined by what we have done with Jesus. When Jesus has been the center of our attention and we have sought to follow Him as faithful disciples, the Church has been strong. But when we have misplaced Him amidst the clutter of our bureaucracy, or relegated Him to a marginal place in our theology, we have been weak and impotent. It's always been true: as goes our relationship with Jesus, so goes the Church.

The earliest Christian creed was, "Jesus is Lord." That is still the best of all the creeds. After all, we call ourselves by his name, "Christians." We consider ourselves to be his disciples. That is how we define ourselves. Like our first century counterparts, we say, "Jesus is Lord." So, if we are, in fact, Christians, Jesus must be the focus of our attention. He must be at the center of our lives. And if He is not, we had better change our name.

In his letter to the Colossians, Paul writes about Jesus. That letter was one of his later books, so it represents a highly developed Christology. As Paul grew older, his way of talking about Jesus did not weaken. It grew stronger. So that, by the time he wrote the letter to the Colossians, he not only thought of Jesus as Savior and Lord, not only as the head of the Church, but as the very truth of God made known in human flesh, the one at the center of all history who holds everything together. Jesus is the one without whom nothing makes sense. He is the one without whom nothing works out. He is the visible image of the invisible God, the truth of God made known to us, the love of God let loose among us to save us and to give us abundant life! Wow! That's extravagant Christology!

There are a great many things we Christians do. There are a great many things we Christians *must* do if we are to be faithful. But the center of it all had better be Jesus. Everything we do must grow out of a life changing encounter with him. Everything we do must receive its direction and motivation from him. He is Lord. He is the head of his body, the Church. So, if we don't start there, with Jesus, nothing is going to go very well.

If we are Christians, there ought to be some good things in our lives which can be explained in no other way than by reference to Jesus. He ought to be that important to us. He can't just be a foot note, a pleasant additive, or a desirable extra. Let me ask you an important question: what is there about your life that it takes Jesus Christ to explain? If you have difficulty coming up with an answer, you had better take a new look at your relationship with him. To say that Jesus is Lord is to move Him from the periphery to the center, to make daily discipleship not optional, but essential. Hear me! Whatever else it may be, authentic Christianity must always be Christ centered!

Emilio Castro, former President of the World Council of Churches, is right on target when he says, "A finger pointing clearly to Jesus, the Lamb of God, is the best gift we have to give to the world today." To be sure, as followers of Jesus, we are to feed the hungry, clothe the naked, educate the illiterate, house the homeless, bind up the wounded, take stands for justice, reach out to the needy, the marginalized, and the outcasts. But even if we do all of that, if we don't bring people into a saving relationship with God, who has made himself known in Jesus, we will have failed to give the world the best we have to give. Because the best gift we have to give to the world is Jesus!

Here is the key: we cannot share Jesus with the world unless we have first claimed Him for ourselves. That is the starting place. I'm talking about a personal, faith-filled, obedient, life-changing relationship with Christ. It's not enough for your grandparents, your parents, your spouse or your friends to have such a relationship. It must be yours: personal, life-changing, on-going, growing, and costly. It must be a relationship at the center of your life, shaping everything else and making everything else more alive and vital. After all, we don't sing, "This is my grand-parents story, this is my mother's song." No, this is *my* story. This is *my* song." It's a personal relationship. Martin Luther used to say, "The heart of Christianity lies in its personal pronouns." So I ask you again: what is there in your life that it takes Jesus Christ to explain? If he's not making a difference, a noticeable difference, what's the point?

Take a look at the world around you. Examine the full sweep of human history. When you get at the essence of it, you will discover that the two greatest realities in the world are these: the heart of God and the hearts of us human beings, and each is ever seeking the other. So much of what we do every day is our search for meaning, our search for connectedness with one another and with God.

Are there days when you feel homesick? Homesick for what, you don't know, but you know the feeling. There is a restlessness, an anxiety. You have a feeling of incompleteness. There is that "God shaped empty place" at the center of life. So much of what we do every day is our attempt to fill the void. It's the search of our hearts for connectedness with the great heart of God.

The good news of the Christian gospel is that we do not search alone. God, too, is searching for us. In fact, the reason we search for God is precisely that God has made us for relationship with Himself. So, we search because we have heard His voice in our depths. We have felt His pull at our lives. And the Bible is the story of our search for God and God's search for us. When you read it with your eyes and your heart wide open, you will see that it is a great love story, the story of longing hearts searching for completeness, searching for connectedness, and searching for relationship.

Throughout the Bible, God reached out to His people. He sent us laws, prophets, priests, messengers of all kinds. He called out to us by His still, small voice. And then, in the fullness of time, God reached out to us in Jesus, the climax of the story, the ultimate expression of God's love for us. The Bible makes the magnificent claim that God Himself drew near to us in Jesus, the Christ. Previous attempts to reach us were not adequate. Something new, something bold, something that would get our attention, something that would touch us in our depths – something like that had to be done. So much does God love us, and so much does God want us to love Him in return that He would go to almost any length to get through to us.

You see, God is not the problem. It is true that we are not the persons we were created to be, and life is not all it is intended to be, but God is not the problem. Some people talk as if God is somehow reluctant to receive us, to forgive us, to claim us as His sons and daughters, and that something had to be done to persuade God or to enable God to do all of that. But I have never believed that. I don't fully understand a God like Jesus showed us. As sinful as we are, as unworthy as we are, for God to love us nevertheless and to claim us as His children, even in our unclean condition – I don't fully understand that, but clearly that is so. And that is why the Christian gospel is such good news!

No, God is not the problem. We are the problem. In this life-long game of hide and seek, the problem is not that God is hiding and we must find Him. No, just the opposite. We have run away from home. We are in hiding, and God must somehow find us and get through to us. So many of us keep thinking that life can be understood in some other way. We keep assuming that life can be found in some other place, so again and again, we run away from God and try to hide.

And century after century, God keeps calling to us, pleading with us, reaching out to us. God keeps calling us home, inviting us into that loving relationship with Himself for which we were created. And Jesus has been God's last, best effort finally to get through to us. The Bible says that Jesus is the promised one, the long expected one. The Jews called Him the Messiah. Christians call Him the Christ. He is the one sent from God to save us and to give us life abundant!

What we Christians affirm is that God accomplished two things in the life, death, and resurrection of Jesus: revelation and redemption.

First, revelation. Jesus is the most perfect revelation of God. Paul wrote, "In Him all the fullness of God was pleased to dwell. He is the visible image of the invisible God." Or, as Jesus put it, "He who has seen me as seen the Father." (John 14:9) So, we don't have to be confused about the nature of

211

God. Look at Jesus and you will know all you need to know about God.

There is a second kind of revelation we see in Jesus. In Him we also see a revelation of what we are intended to be. Look at Jesus and you will see what God had in mind when we were created. Look at Jesus' love, his compassion, his servanthood, and his trusting obedience. Look at all of that and you will see what Christian discipleship should look like for us. Revelation.

Revelation is important. All I know about God and all I know about authentic humanness I have learned from Jesus. But, as important as that is, there is something even more important. God acted in Jesus' life not only for revelation, but also for redemption. Through Jesus, God has reached out to all who have wandered away in order to call us home, to forgive us, to restore us to our intended place as the sons and daughters of God. In Jesus, we are introduced to the immense dimensions of God's love. In Jesus, we see just how far God will go to reach out to us and to bring us back to Himself.

Do you know what I fear? I fear that we have heard this story so many times that we have become rather blasé about it. We have become anesthetized, so the shock of the gospel has not gotten through to us. Having tried so many things throughout history to reach us, almost in desperation God did something utterly new, something radical in the whole history of religion. In Jesus, there are two things that are new, at least in emphasis.

First, in Jesus we meet a God who takes the initiative and seeks us out. God doesn't wait for us to come to Him. In God's great Father's love, He comes to us. He is the shepherd who goes out in the night seeking the one sheep who is lost. He is the father out there on the road, running to meet his wayward son, arms of love and forgiveness and welcome opened wide. That is God, according to Jesus. God is the One who seeks us. That's new.

And, a vulnerable God, a suffering God. That's new too. We've heard before about a holy God, a righteous God, a powerful God, even a loving God. But a God who loves enough to suffer – that's new. You see, genuine love makes us vulnerable. When we love, we become so close to our loved one that we suffer with them and we suffer for them, and God is no exception. And, for the life of me, I can't think of a more powerful, more redemptive expression of love than a love willing to suffer, to give up its own life on behalf of the one who is loved. What more can you do than that?

I remember the account of a child who was trapped in a burning building. When his father realized that his son was still inside the blazing structure, he went running back inside, wrapped the boy in a rug, and brought him out to safety. But, in the process, his hands and arms were burned and permanently scarred. Later, as an adult, the son said, "If I am ever tempted to doubt my father's love for me, all I have to do is look at his hands."

That works for me too. Whenever I am tempted to doubt God's love for me, all I have to do is to look at Jesus, the visible image of the invisible God. Particularly I look at Jesus upon the cross. I see the suffering love there and I remember that "God loved the world so much that He gave His only son." (John 3:16) What more can He do to get through to us, to wrap His arms of love around us than that?

And, have you ever thought about the exclamation point God places after the crucifixion? If Jesus' death were not enough to show us His love, God goes one better and sends

213

Jesus back after the resurrection! God sent His son back to the very ones who had denied him, deserted him, and crucified him. Talk about love going the second mile!

Think about that and see if you can wrap your mind and heart around such love. I couldn't have done it. If I had sent my son to some people to tell them how much I care, and they had taken my son and betrayed him, forsaken him, ridiculed him, tortured him, and finally killed him – if they had done that to my son and delivered his dead body to me – if in some way I could have breathed life back into him, do you think I would send him back to those people? Not on your life! It's hard to imagine a love like that.

Listen! The gospel says that God loves us so much that, after restoring Jesus to life, God sent His son back again. God sent Him back to the soldiers who had crucified Him to say, "You're forgiven." God sent Him back to Peter who had denied Him to say, "Peter, you're forgiven." God sent Him back to the disciples who had forsaken Him to say, "You're forgiven. Now, you go tell the whole world that they're forgiven. Tell them that I want them to be my sons and daughters. Baptize them and bring them to Me because I love them so."

Do you understand? Even after all the world did to Jesus, God still sent Him back because of His great love. If that doesn't get to you, nothing will. If that doesn't melt your heart, nothing will. If that doesn't make you experience God's love for you, I don't know what more God can do. God loved the world so much that He gave His son, not once but twice!

Let me underline it like this: It happened years ago. It was the week that Harry Reasoner had died. On Sunday night I was at home after a busy Sunday schedule. I was trying to unwind by sitting in my favorite chair, flipping through the television channels to see what was on. I settled on "Sixty Minutes," where they were doing a tribute to the CBS news commentator, Harry Reasoner, who had died that week. It was a touching piece, lovingly put together. They showed film clips of Harry's life, particularly his television career. His fellow journalists had difficulty controlling their emotions as they narrated and made comments. As usual, Andy Rooney had the last word.

I listened to what Andy said and I wrote it down, almost verbatim. He said, "Harry Reasoner was the most brilliant correspondent to be on television. But he did some dumb things too. Otherwise he would never have died at the age of sixty-eight. How else do you explain the fact that a man who had already lost a lung to cancer continued to smoke two packs of cigarettes a day?" Andy concluded, "I'm sad, but I'm angry too. Harry was so careless with our affection for him."

I heard those words and immediately I thought, "That's us! That's what we do to God!" Day after day, year after year God blesses us, calls to us, and reaches out to us. Finally, God sends His love to us through Jesus' life and his death upon the cross. But so many hear the story of that and continue to do business as usual. So many hear the story of that and keep on living as if it had never happened. We are so careless with that greatest of all loves!

The Bible says that "God shows His love for us in that while we were still sinners, Christ died for us." (Romans 5:8) Surely if you hear that, surely if you understand that, you will respond to God's love by loving Him in return. Surely you will...surely you will...because I honestly don't know what more God can do!

There is a song that says it:

"O how He loves you and me. O how He loves you
    and me.
He gave His life, what more can He give?
O how He loves you. O how He loves me.
O how He loves you and me!"

Prayer: Father, such a great love calls for our love in return.
Don't let us turn a deaf ear to Your call. Don't let us be
careless with Your love. Help us here and now to say, "Yes"
to You. Call us to Yourself by the power of Your great love
made known to us in Jesus. In his name we pray. Amen.

One Nation Under God

Psalms 33:8-22

It was during the Eisenhower administration that the words, "under God" were added to the pledge of allegiance. As a result, we now say, "One nation, under God, indivisible, with liberty and justice for all."

Years before, President Lincoln sounded that same note. In his Gettysburg Address Lincoln said, "We here highly resolve that these dead shall not have died in vain, that this nation, under God, shall have a new birth of freedom, and that government of the people, by the people, for the people, shall not perish from the earth." Historians tell us that those words, "under God" were not in Lincoln's first draft of the speech. But, in a moment of inspiration, he added them as he was giving the address. Then, he considered them to be so important that he included them in every subsequent draft of the speech. President Lincoln thought it important that we acknowledge being "under God." The Psalmist was expressing the same idea in different words when he wrote, "Blessed is the nation whose God is the Lord."

If those words, "under God" are only incidental, if they are merely a sentimental "nod to God," then they are not worth our attention. But if they are to be taken seriously, if our national purpose is indeed to be a "nation under God," then those words and what they mean may be the most important part of our national heritage. So, that's what I want us to think about. What does it mean to be "a nation under God"? What was the Psalmist talking about when he said, "Blessed is the nation whose God is the Lord"?

The first thing to see is that we are in fact under God whether we know that or not and whether we approve of that or not. God is God after all – always has been and always will be – and God is in charge in this world. All through the Bible there is a constantly recurring theme. There is warning after warning about the temptation which has always plagued people and nations, and that is the temptation to run things in our own way, as if we are god, giving little thought to the way God wants things done.

The fact is, however, that there is a moral law at work in history. God has established that moral law because God wants the world to go in a certain direction. And the person or the nation who ignores that, or who refuses to cooperate with that, sooner or later comes to destruction. A life lived going against the grain of God's intentions gathers a great many splinters! It just doesn't work very well. If we want to be successful, fulfilled, and happy, we must do it God's way. If we want to build enduringly, we must build on the foundation of God's will, because God is in charge here, whether we know it or not, and whether we approve of it or not!

The best evidence I know of the existence of God is what begins to happen when it is denied. The person or the nation who takes things in hand with no thought of God's purposes is soon in trouble. The scriptures put it like this: "Do not be deceived; God is not mocked, for you reap whatever you sow." (Galatians 6:11) That applies to individuals and nations alike. Of course, we can take what we want in life. We can make choices and live our lives in whatever ways we choose. We are free to do that. But if we choose the way of unrighteousness, if we reject established moral values, and live the grasping life, the self-centered life, if we live as if God doesn't even exist, then let us not be surprised when the bills start to come in. Read books of history, read the front page of any newspaper, and you will hear the same word being shouted in unmistakable language: "Don't be deceived; God is not mocked, for you reap whatever you sow."

Just look at the collapse of the great Roman Empire. Look at the fall of the Berlin wall. Look at South Africa with the failure of apartheid. Look at the former Soviet Union with the dismantling of that totalitarian system. Look at the demise of slavery and the passage of women's suffrage. History is on the side of freedom because God is on the side of freedom. Soon or late, those systems that oppress people will be washed down the drain of history. And those systems that affirm the worth and dignity of all people, those systems that are on the side of truth, justice, and righteousness will win the day. It is never quickly enough, according to our timetables. Sometimes it is slow going because God has given us freedom, even the freedom to get in God's way. But it will happen. Write it down. It will happen because God is finally in charge in this world. Whether we know it or not, whether we approve of it or not, we are, in fact, under God. That's the first thing I want to say.

The second thing for us to see is that something good happens to the individual and the nation who not only acknowledges that we are "under God," but also celebrates that. We not only say, "That's the way it is." We also say, "That's the way we want it! We want to be 'a nation under God.'"

219

When we have been at our best, that's been true of us as Americans. The founders of this nation did not create a government and then begin to decide what kind of government it would be. No, they began with a faith in God. That produced in them a concern for certain values. The government, then, came into being in order to secure and protect those values. But the foundation of it all was and is faith in God.

The founders of this nation believed in a God Who created all that is. They believed that God had a plan in mind, and that God created everything to fit together harmoniously as a part of that plan. They believed that life works out best when we try to understand God's plan and then cooperate with it. Life just doesn't work out very well when we try to go against God's plan. According to God's plan, every human being is a child of God, and is therefore of infinite worth, every human being. And, every human being has certain rights, rights given not by the state, but by God. And because these rights were not given by the state, the state must not attempt to take them away.

In America, the nation is not intended to be the master of the people. The nation is intended to be the servant of the people. The whole purpose of government is to protect and guarantee the rights given to the people by God. That belief is woven into the fabric of our nation's history. Read again those magnificent words from our Declaration of Independence: "We hold these truths to be self-evident, that all men are created equal, that they are endowed by their creator with certain unalienable rights, that among these are life, liberty, and the pursuit of happiness. That to secure these rights, governments are instituted among men, deriving their just powers from the consent of the governed."

I believe those words are among the greatest ever put on paper. But when they were written those ideals were not all reality, they were a dream of what should and can be. Even the writers were talking about a future that they did not fully understand. When they used the word, "men," they should have said, "all people." At that time in history women could not vote, own property, run for office, or sue for divorce. And, when they talked about "all men are created equal," many of them owned slaves. That term, "equality" is often misunderstood. I have heard people say that those words are ridiculous because all people are not created equal. And, in one sense they are right. I was not born with a silver spoon in my mouth. Growing up in a preacher's family, I was on the edge of poverty. Other families were wealthier than us. And, I found it far easier to make "A's" in the classroom than did many of my classmates. We were not equal in that sense. I have always loved sports, but I was always among the slowest and skinniest of my classmates, and often the last chosen when dividing up into teams. We are not all created equal in those senses, but that is not what the founders were talking about. They were talking about equality of worth in the eyes of God and in the eyes of the nation because all are created as the sons and daughters of God. That equality of worth gives equality of rights as well, rights given by God. All of that represents a dream of the way things should and can be, something to work for, as we seek to become "a more perfect union." We have, through struggle, pain, and tears, achieved some aspects of that dream. Slavery was abolished. Women and children were given additional rights under the law. We have made some progress in racial justice, although we still have more to do. We still have work to do in women's rights, gender equality, issues of national origin, and others. But America has always been about the dream!

Part of the dream is to be "e pluribus unum." We are to be "one nation, under God, indivisible." But today we are

221

more divided than at any time in my memory. I am saddened by the number of powerful people who seek to divide us, to separate us for political or financial gain. That is what totalitarian governments do, because a divided people are easier to manipulate and control than are unified people. When we are at our best, our strongest, we are "one nation, indivisible." I was a child during World War II. I have vivid memories of those things we collected and took to school: newspapers, tin cans, aluminum foil, rubber bands, etc. I remember ration books by which we all sacrificed for the common good. I remember stars in neighbors' windows, representing sons and daughters lost in war. I remember all of us scraping money together to buy savings bonds. At that point in my life I had never heard the words, "Republican," "Democrat," "Independent." I knew nothing of politics. But I knew, I felt it in my depths, that all of us together were Americans! That felt good!

I remember watching on television, after the attacks of 9/11, our President stood in the rubble of the twin towers, representing us all, and declaring our oneness. Democrats, Republicans, and Independents were not attacked, Americans were attacked. We were together, unified, and it felt good, didn't it? We must remember every hour of every day that the things that unite us are far more numerous and far more important that anything that might divide us. When we are at our best, we are "one nation under God, indivisible, with liberty and justice for all."

I love the fact that our founders insisted that certain rights are absolute, not given by the state, and not taken away by the state. They are ours because our basic rights have been given to us by God. Listen to Jefferson: "The God who gave us life gave us liberty at the same time." Our nation is about freedom, about rights, given not by the state, but given by God!

The study of history is so important, and I grieve that so few of us understand much of it. We dare not forget the dreams that gave us birth. Do you know why the "Bill of Rights" is so important? Sometimes we say, flippantly, "A democracy is where the people vote and the majority rules." But that's not all there is to our democracy. Many if not most of the early settlers in this country were religious minorities, ethnic minorities, political minorities, who came to this land to get away from oppressive majorities. They knew what it was like to have the will of the majority imposed upon them by force. So, remembering that, they built into the structures of this country a protection of certain rights which they called "unalienable," rights which even a majority could not take away, because our founders believed that those rights had been given to them by God. Among these rights are the right to vote, the right to worship or not to worship according to one's conscience, the right to assemble peaceably to express grievances, the right to free speech, the right to a free press (there cannot be democracy without a free press), the right to be secure in our homes, the right to trial by a jury of our peers – those kinds of rights.

Remember the lessons of history when we are tempted to change or ignore the Bill of Rights. Remember the lessons of history when we are tempted to run roughshod over some small group. Remember that our founders feared oppressive majorities! There are certain unalienable rights which belong to all people because those rights were given to us by God.

Where did all of that come from? There is no way to understand our nation and its history apart from our spiritual roots. The values which make our nation great have come from our faith in God. And if we ever abandon our faith, those values will disappear as well. Destroy a root and sooner or later all that has grown up from it will die. The greatness of our nation springs from its spiritual roots, and if we allow those roots to wither and die, any lingering greatness will soon follow. Write this down in your consciousness and never forget it: democracy and faith are intertwined. In the long sweep of history it is difficult to have one without the other.

A totalitarian state is made possible only by the denial of a higher allegiance. It is so tempting and so dangerous to give up our freedom to the control of a few. The state comes first. The beloved leader demands first loyalty. And when a dictator takes over, he first seeks control of the press and radio and television in order to control the flow of information. That's why freedom of the press is essential in a democracy! In all lasting democracies, it is recognized that above the authority of the state is the authority of God. It is from God that we get the values that make democracy possible. And it is from God that we receive the grace and strength to pursue those values. So, democracy and faith must work together. It's a package deal!

What I am talking about is certainly not a new issue. In the New Testament the issue is raised: who gets first allegiance, Caesar or God? The first Christians were willing to pray for Caesar, but they were not willing to burn incense on his altar. And many of them were put to death because they refused to give to Caesar that which belonged to God. Over and over again, throughout history, the state has tried to claim an allegiance that should belong only to God, and the best Christians have kept getting into trouble by insisting that governments as well as individuals are accountable to God and come under God's judgement. Surely we understand by now that the person who loves his country best is not the one who approves of it no matter what is done, but the one who consistently calls his country to live up to the best that we know.

In the sixteenth century, Sir Thomas More was put to death by King Henry VIII. More refused to obey the King when, according to his conscience, it meant disobeying God. He went to his death saying, "I am the King's good servant, but God's first." I think he was the King's best servant precisely because he was God's servant first. Listen! The most valuable citizens are neither the unloving critics nor the uncritical lovers, but those who love their country enough to insist upon the highest standards. They love their country best because they love God first!

A number of court cases through the years have dealt with this issue. The Andersonville Trial after the Civil War, the Nuremburg Trials after World War II, the Adolf Eichman Trial, and more recently the War Crimes Tribunal dealing with crimes in the Balkans, have all come to the same conclusion: even a nation is subject to a higher authority. It is not enough to say, "I was ordered to do it," or "My job required it." A nation cannot demand absolute obedience, because that is an authority that belongs only to God.

During the most intense period of the Civil War, someone came to President Lincoln and said, "I surely hope the Lord is on our side." Lincoln replied, "I am not at all concerned about that because I know the Lord is always on the side of right. But it is my constant anxiety and prayer that both I and this nation will be on the Lord's side." That is precisely what has made our nation great. When we have been at our best, we have known that we are a nation under God, and we have said that is the way we want it. We want to bring our values, our policies, and our actions under the sovereignty of God, because that is what is best for all of God's children. We gladly choose to be a nation under God, guided by God, dependent upon God, and accountable to God.

Of course, and this is the third thing, the good news is that as we willingly place ourselves under God, we discover that God's arms of love and strength are under us, sustaining us, holding us up. I return again and again to those magnificent words of Isaiah: "They who wait upon the Lord shall renew their strength, they shall mount up with wings as eagles, they shall run and not be weary, they shall walk and not faint." (Isaiah 40:31) That is true of nations no less than of individuals.

Throughout the history of our nation we have had a sense that God is with us, not with us as over against other nations, or with us to the neglect of other nations, but as we have placed our trust in God, we have sensed that God has been with us, and that God's grace and strength are sufficient for our every need. God's providence has seen us through war and disease and famine and flood and depression. God has been with us through struggles without and within. Steadfastly, dependably, God has been with us, never abandoning us or forsaking us. And, by God's grace we have not only endured, we have prospered!

There is no mistaking it: as a nation, we have been richly blessed by God. Again, not that God prefers us to other nations, or that God has blessed us in a way He is unwilling to do for others. It's just that ours is a heritage of faith, and when you honor God by your faith and seek to bring your ways into harmony with God's will, that is the way of life that leads to blessings. That can happen in any nation where God is honored and God's will is done. That's the way it is because that's the way God has created the world to work.

We must know that to be blessed in the Biblical sense is not so much to be given special privilege as it is to be given special responsibility. We are blessed by God not so that we can indulge ourselves, but so that we can be used by God to accomplish God's purposes. That's why our founders believed that the dream God has given to us, the dream of freedom and justice and righteousness, was not just for us. No, we who believe in the dream are to be "a light to the nations." Or, as Lincoln described us, "the last, best hope of earth." Or, as President Reagan referred to us as "the shining city on the hill." Clearly, we are blessed by God so that we can then be a blessing to the whole world!

Let me underline it like this: during the Protestant Reformation, when tensions were great and the very lives of the reformers were at stake, an enemy of Martin Luther said to him, "Tell me, when the whole world turns against you, church, state, princes, people, where will you be then?" Luther calmly replied, "Why, then as now, I'll be in the hands of almighty God." And so are we.

We are a nation under God. That's the way it is, and that's the way we want it, because our God is good, and loving, and powerful. And there is no more secure place to be than in the hands of a God like that. That's what the Psalmist meant when he wrote, "Blessed is the nation whose God is the Lord."

One final story. Do you remember the anxiety experienced by so many as we turned the corner into the 21st century? We talked a great deal about Y2K and I had many people call me for counselling. An earlier generation experienced many of the same emotions as they moved into the 20th century. In the midst of their anxiety, it was announced that at the stroke of midnight, December 31, 1899, Edward Everett Hale was to speak on the Commons in Boston. The square was crowded with people, eager to hear this brilliant and respected preacher/orator as they began the new century. A hush fell over the crowd as he made his way to the rostrum. There, with the wind whipping his robe, he opened his mouth to speak, and this is what he said: "Lord, Thou hast been our dwelling place in all generations. Before the mountains were brought forth, or ever Thou hadst formed the earth and the world, even from everlasting to everlasting, Thou art God."

And with that, he turned and left the rostrum. That was his speech, simply and magnificently that. Let it be mine as well. We can look to the future with hope if we will remember the source of our dreams, allow those dreams to be born anew in us, and send our roots deep into the greatness of God. That's what it means to be one nation under God!

Prayer: God of our fathers and our mothers, God of our children and grandchildren, and our God: we acknowledge that You are God, and in trust we place ourselves and our nation in Your loving and strong hands. Make straight what is crooked in us. Heal what is broken in us. Give us a renewed dream of who we can be as Your sons and daughters, and then, by Your grace, enable us to make that dream come true. Enable us to be one nation, under God, indivisible, with liberty and justice for all. Amen.

You Can Depend Upon It

Psalms 90: 1-2

I'm the kind of person who likes things to be neat, orderly, dependable. I suppose I am a true child of Wesley, because I like things to be well organized. I am most comfortable with a methodical approach to any task. In some ways you might even say I am finicky. I attempt to pull together the fragmented parts of my life through the use of some kind of routine.

For example, I sleep on the same side of the bed every night. I enjoy beginning the day by going out to find the morning newspaper lying reliably in the driveway where it's supposed to be. If you were to look in my bathroom drawer, you would find my hairbrush, toothpaste, toothbrush, and a varied assortment of other toiletries, all arranged in precise order. And woe be to him or her who rearranges the order! My children have teased me for years about the way I eat. Whether I am slicing a watermelon, cutting a steak, or preparing a baked potato for the first bite, I go about it with the intensity and precision of a surgeon's scalpel. My idea of a nightmare is to be standing before a large congregation and discover that I forgot to put on my pants or neglected to prepare a sermon. (I can hardly wait to hear what you amateur psychologists do with that one.)

I think you get the idea. I don't like surprises very much. I like cars that start, checks that don't bounce, watches that run, promises that are kept. The bottom line is that I want to know what I can count on! My guess is that you do too.

And that's the problem. For no matter how much we try to structure our lives... no matter how diligently we seek to reduce the risk... the fact is that there is so much in life that is undependable. The weather is certainly undependable. We tend to take good weather for granted, but then we plan a picnic, a day of golf, a trip to the beach, and all of a sudden it begins to rain. There is no predicting it. There is no controlling it. It's undependable.

Health is undependable. We may be sailing along in great condition when suddenly for no explainable reason we are knocked flat on our backs. No one is assured of good health or long life. It's all risky.

The economy is certainly undependable. Take any two authoritative economists, sit them down at a table, and in five minutes they will be arguing. Investing your money is always a guessing game. Who knows what the future will bring. Uncertainty, undependability in the market place. I'll say there is!

Most people enjoy being in a familiar environment, being surrounded by people and things that we know and love. Yet, that's undependable too. While living in California, one year on vacation we took our family to Atlanta where Patricia and I spent our first married years. But as we drove around our nostalgia turned to sadness and our sadness turned almost to anger. Because it is no longer the way it was! All our favorite eating places are gone. We could hardly find our way to Emory University because everything is changed. The once familiar is now unfamiliar. It has become a truism that you

230

can't go home again. Because of the pervasiveness of change, what was is no more. The familiar settings and environs of life are undependable.

Sadly, people are often undependable. Those we depend upon, those we love die or move away. Or they disappoint us, reject us, hurt us. That, perhaps is the greatest hurt of all... to really trust someone, to count on someone and then to have them disappoint us. That hurts, doesn't it?

I could go on and on, but you get the point. There is so much in life that is undependable. I remember a song from my high school years that sought to express that sentiment. I can hear it now, in the nasal twang of a hillbilly voice, half singing half saying:

> "The tin roof leaks and the chimney leans,
> And there's a hole in the seat of my ole blue jeans,
> And I've et the last of the pork and beans...
> Cain't depend on nuthin'."

I have days when I feel like that, and I'll be you do too And yet we need something in our life that's dependable. Every human being does. There is no stability to life if everything is changeable and if everything is constantly up for grabs. Unless we know where true North is on the compass, we don't know where anything else is. There must be some reliable point of reference, or else life has no meaning. There must be some stable foundation on which to stand. There must be something meaningful from which everything else derives its meaning. There must be something, somewhere that we can depend upon. There must be... mustn't there?

For generations, Christians have affirmed that in the midst of so much undependability, there is One we can depend upon... there is One who is utterly deserving of our

231

trust... there is One who is steadfast and reliable... that One is God!

God is not one kind of God one day and another kind the next. He does not provide for us one day and neglect us the next. He does not love us one day and forsake us the next. No! Above all others, God is the One who is utterly dependable. "From everlasting to everlasting, God is God!"

When I say that, I'm not talking about mere wishful thinking. The providence of God, the steadfastness of God, the dependability of God... that's been the experience of God's people across thousands of years of history. It's not fantasy. It's not mere theory. It's experience! We are able to trust God because we have experienced Him to be trustworthy!

So, if you want to know what you can depend upon, there is only one answer I can give with any degree of confidence. You can depend upon God! Now I want to say three things about that.

I.

First, God will never let us down. You can depend upon that. God will never let us down. One of the major themes of the Bible is God's steadfast love. God is not against us. He is for us. He is with us in every experience of life, seeking to provide for our needs, working with the raw material of life to bring something good out of whatever happens.

Jesus said of God, "He makes His sun to shine on the evil and on the good, and sends His rain on the just and on the unjust." Regularly, dependably, God provides for all our needs.

Of course, He doesn't provide for all our wants. And that's why it sometime seems as if God is letting us down. All too many people think of God as their own private utility, in business to cater to their whims and fulfill their desires. Their prayer, if they were honest would be, "Not Thy will, but mine be done."

I heard a story recently which reminded me of our childlike inclinations. A mother became concerned because her son away at college would not write. She wrote several times a week begging him to write, but he never got around to it. She complained to her brother about it. After thinking for a few moments, the brother made a small wager that he could get the boy to write in less than a week. He wrote a brief note, placing a postscript at the bottom saying, "In case you are running short on cash I am enclosing a ten dollar bill." But he failed to enclose the money. In the next mail he had an answer. "Dear Uncle Willie: About that ten dollars..."

Isn't that just like so many of us? In our self-centeredness, we are interested in God only as long as He is giving us what we want. But the first time we are disappointed, the first time we are hurt, we are through with God, the Church, religion, the whole bit. It's true. There are times when we feel that God has let us down. Even Jesus felt it: "My God, my God, why hast Thou forsaken me?"

Listen, let's understand once and for all what God's promise to us is. He never promised to give us everything we ask for. He never promised to make us healthy, wealthy, wise and happy. That's not the promise. There will be times in life when we will be hurt, disappointed, confused, despairing. Those experiences come to every human being and to go through them doesn't mean that God has let us down.

The promise is that in every experience of life, we are not alone, God is with us. He shares our hurts. He provides what we need. He gives strength equal to the struggle. And He uses His powerful and loving hands to twist and shape the disappointments of life into something good. "God is our refuge and strength, a very present help in trouble."

Not what you want, but what you need, God will supply. You can depend upon it!

II.

A second thing must also be said. Though God's love never lets us down, it also never lets us off. We can be sure that God takes sin seriously. There is a moral law which God enforces with the same strength and dependability with which He provides for our needs.

So many soft-headed people confuse love with weakness. Let me assure you that God's love is not weak. It has backbone. Don't make the mistake of assuming that because God loves you, you can get by with anything. Just the opposite. Precisely because God loves us, He won't let us get by with just anything. It's true that God is compassionate towards sinners. But you'd better believe that he's not complacent about sin.

Our foreparents used to talk a great deal about sin and punishment. Such language has pretty much gone out of our vocabulary. But unless we stop thinking of God as some sort of indulgent, celestial grandfather, who winks playfully at our sins and who is so busy loving us that He is indifferent to our behavior... unless we get away from such fuzzy, unbiblical thinking, we may have to start talking about sin and punishment again.

234

Jonathan Edwards, centuries ago, preached a famous sermon which he called, "Sinners In the Hands of an Angry God." He spoke in such graphic terms that the members of the congregation felt themselves hanging by a thread over the pit of hell, the flames licking at their heels. Women fainted and strong men clung to the pillars of the Church in fear.

Now that's overdone, and I certainly wouldn't want to return to that. But the concept of the fear of God is not all bad. God has written certain laws into the fabric of human life and if we violate those laws there are consequences. The scriptures say it: "Be not deceived, God is not mocked. Whatever a person sows, that shall he also reap." We would do well to fear the anger of a righteous God! Because He will not let us off.

It's true that God loves us. It's also true that God is always ready to forgive us. There is no sin so great that God will not forgive. He will cut us free from the guilt of our sin and enable us to start all over again. But God does not exempt us from the consequences of our deeds. I hope you will hear and understand that. The consequences of our actions remain. What we sow we reap!

You go to a party. You drink too much. Driving home you have an accident and an innocent person is killed. God will forgive you for that. He will cut you free from the guilt of that. But He will not do away with the consequences. The innocent victim is still dead. God will not let you off. Sin always results in suffering.

I suppose there are those who would say that if God really loves us, He wouldn't let us do hurtful things. He would spare us from the painful consequences of our deeds. But to me, that's one of the primary evidences of God's strong and wise love, because it is an indication of the fact

235

that God takes us seriously. Our freedom means something. We are not puppets on a string. We make real choices and something vital is at stake in those choices. Our decisions make life good or they make life miserable. But they are our choices. They are real! There is no virtue in making the right choice unless there is also the guilt when we make the wrong one.

Don't you see that life takes on larger dimensions when we understand that the moral law is dependable? God has given us freedom and we are accountable to Him for what we do with our freedom. There is an old story to the effect that Daniel Webster was once asked what was the greatest idea that had ever crossed his mind. The famous statesman is said to have replied, "The fact that I must someday stand before almighty God and render unto Him an account of my life." That a pretty big idea! It's an ennobling idea. We are responsible, we are accountable to God!

God is a Father whose love never lets us down. But He is also a Father whose love cannot let us off.

III.

One final thing must be said. God will never let us down. God will never let us off. And most importantly, God will never let us go.

I think that's the greatest word which can be said about love — it keeps on loving in spite of everything. No matter how often it is disappointed… no matter how often it is rejected… no matter how often it is wounded… no matter how far the loved one wanders… love always holds on, never gives up, never lets go.

That's very reassuring to me. The gospel really becomes good news when it finally sinks into my consciousness that there is absolutely nothing that I can do to make God stop loving me. That's beyond my capability. No matter what I've done, no matter where I've been, the one overriding, redeeming reality about my life is that I am loved by God! I can accept that or I can reject that, but nothing can ever change that! And that's the gospel.

Let me say it like this: There was a son who was everything his father didn't want him to be. He was rebellious, irresponsible, irreverent. He was kicked out of school. He ran up debts and almost bankrupted the family. He broke every rule in the book, drifting in and out of jail. Time and again the father bailed him out of trouble. It almost killed the old man. Seeing the toll all of this was taking on a very loving man, a friend said to him one day: "How much more can you do? You've done more than your share already. I tell you, if he were my boy I'd let him go." The old man smiled and said, "If he were your boy I would too, but he's my boy, and I can never let him go." Do you hear the good news in that? God is our Father, and He will never let us go! What we have been talking about is something we desperately need to remember. So let me say it one more time as together we underline it in red...

One of my favorite writers tells about the time when he was a young minister and had as a close friend a professor of music. He loved to visit the instructor at his studio for he never failed to get a lift from the contact. One day he went to see his musician friend, and when he answered the door, the young minister said, "What's the good news today?" Without saying a word, the professor walked to one corner of the room, picked up a mallet, and firmly struck a tuning bar which was hanging there. Then he turned to his young friend and said: "That, my friend, is the note 'A.' It was 'A' yesterday. It will be 'A' tomorrow and for a hundred years. The soprano next door may warble off key. The tenor upstairs may flat his high ones. But that, my friend is 'A'."

There is so much in life that is changeable and undependable. That's why I celebrate the affirmation that "from everlasting to everlasting (God) is God." He will never let us down. He will never let us off. And He will never let us go. You can depend upon that! And I think that's good news!

Prayer: God our Father, we are grateful that whatever we need You are willing to supply. In the midst of change, You are changeless. In the midst of uncertainty, You are dependable. Now come to us Father, and give meaning and direction to our lives because we have been touched by the strength and the steadfastness of Your love. In the Master's name we pray. Amen.

How Can I Say Thanks?

I Thessalonians 5:16-18

There are a great many songs that I love, many of which have left indelible marks upon my life. I will never forget one by Andre Crouch which I heard for the first time as my daughter, Lynne, sang it in worship one Sunday. Absorb the words:

> "How can I say thanks for the things you have done
>   for me?
> Things so undeserved, yet you gave to prove your
>   love for me;
> The voices of a million angels could not express my
>   gratitude.
> All that I am and ever hope to be, I owe it all to thee.
>
> With his blood He has saved me, with his power He
>   has raised me,
> To God be the glory for the things He has done."

There are few questions in life more important than, "How can I say thanks?" That question has compelled me to write about it. To begin with, in the Bible, thanksgiving is more than compiling an inventory of blessings. I remember the old gospel song we used to sing in my growing up years: "Count your blessings, name them one by one, and it will

239

surprise you what the Lord has done." That's a good thing to do, to count blessings, as long as it doesn't stop there. The danger is that we will look at life moment by moment, and let our circumstances determine whether or not we are grateful. We look at something and we might say, "This is a blessing. I thank God for this." Then we look at something else and say, "That is a bummer. I'm not grateful for that." So, gratitude is reduced to a sometimes thing, on again, off again. That is what happens when gratitude is reduced to making an inventory of blessings.

Instead of that, the Bible insists that thanksgiving should be a way of life. It is an attitude of the heart, and it should be continuous. In his first letter to the Thessalonians, Paul said: "Rejoice always...Give thanks in all circumstances." Do you understand? When we approach it in the right way, thanksgiving is not an inventory of blessings, it is an attitude of the heart.

A person with the attitude of gratitude understands that all of life is a gift. So much of life is beautiful, joyful, meaning filled. That is evidence of God's extravagant love for us. For example, God did not have to create a world of color. It could all have been dull gray. God could have made just one kind of tree or flower, or none at all, instead of the rich variety we enjoy. God could have put but one star in the sky. God could have made all sunsets alike. God did not have to create a world of such rich variety. But such is the generosity of God that, as long as we live, we will be experiencing newness, new sights, new sounds, new tastes, new smells, and new experiences. Open your eyes, indeed open all your senses, and experience God's world abundantly filled with God's blessings.

Think about the fact that you and I did not have to be. The fact that we are rather than are not should be a reason to be grateful for everything that follows. Even the difficult times of life can be occasions of gratitude, because the capacity to experience pain and disappointment and sorrow are better than not experiencing anything.

One of the things I am most grateful for is my capacity to be thankful, because when I am thankful, I continually find more things to be thankful for. And, when God's blessings are received with gratitude, somehow they are enlarged, and the experience of them is enriched.

How impoverished are those people who are not thankful. I think about the man who said, "Why should I thank God for something I worked so hard to acquire?" He just doesn't understand, and I am sorry for him. The person unable to feel gratitude has a shriveled up heart. Paul asked the key question: "What do you have that you did not receive?" Think about that. What do you have that you did not receive? Everything good in life we have received. And all of us who are people of faith know that when you trace all good things back to their source, finally they have all come from God, from God's fatherly love for all God's children. Maltbie Babcock understood. He wrote:

> "Back of the loaf is the snowy flour, and back of the
> flour, the mill;
> And back of the mill is the wheat and the shower and
> the sun and the Father's will."

The more we understand that, the more we become aware of just how many blessings there are, and the more we are able to allow them to enrich our lives.

I repeat: thanksgiving more than just taking inventory. It is an outlook, an attitude of the heart. It's the old idea, "Is the glass half full or half empty?" Obviously, your answer depends upon your point of view, your heart's attitude toward all of life. It is has become abundantly clear to me that what you look for in life, you tend to find. The person who sees the glass half full will always be more aware of blessings than the person who sees it half empty. In fact, we might even say that you have to be grateful before you are able clearly to see all the blessings for which to be grateful. It's an attitude.

John Wesley learned it as a student at Oxford University. A young man knocked on his door one night and asked to speak to him. After some conversation, Wesley noticed the man's thin coat. He was concerned because it was a cold winter's night. Wesley suggested that he had better get another coat. The young man replied, "This is the only coat I have, and I thank God for it." Wesley asked him if he had yet eaten dinner. He replied, "I have had nothing today but water to drink, but I thank God for that." Wesley began to be uneasy in the young man's presence. He reminded him that he had better get to his room soon, lest he be locked out. "Then what would you have to thank God for?" Wesley asked. "Then I will thank him," replied the man, "that I have dry stones to lie upon tonight."

Wesley was moved by what he heard, and said to him, "You thank God when you have nothing to wear, nothing to eat, and no bed to lie on. What else do you thank God for?" He replied, "I thank God that He has given me life, and a heart to love him, and a desire to serve him." That young man left Wesley's apartment with a coat from Wesley's closet, some money for food, and words of appreciation for the witness he had made. Later, Wesley wrote in his journal, "I shall never forget that man. He convinced me that there is something in religion to which I am a stranger."

Isn't that amazing? In so many ways he was deprived. In so many ways life was difficult for him. And yet, he found it in his heart to be thankful. That's what Paul was getting at: "Give thanks in all circumstances." Get that: all circumstances. It's not just an inventory of blessings, it's an attitude of the heart.

St. John of the Cross once said, "One act of thanksgiving made when things go wrong is worth a thousand when things go well." That gets at the Biblical approach to thanksgiving, doesn't it? Biblical thanksgiving is a way of life, an attitude of the heart. It finds a way to thank God for his presence, his grace, his blessings, and his strength, even in the difficult times of life.

My mother helped me to understand something of that. My mother probably was a more powerful influence upon my life than anyone else. Growing up on a farm, with a large family, then marrying a preacher and living in a parsonage, she never had much money or material possessions. She lost her first child in an influenza epidemic, in which she almost lost her life as well. The parsonages we lived in were often not in good condition. I well remember, during rain, going through the house putting all the pots and pans we owned beneath the leaks in the roof. Yet, she never complained. She just did whatever was necessary. Through it all was that beatific smile. And I heard her quote Paul on countless occasions – it may have been one of her favorite Bible verses, "I have learned in whatever state I am, to be content." (Philippians 4:11 KJV)

After my father died, I visited my mother in the nursing home. There, almost totally blind and deaf, she continued to be "content." One day I asked her how she was. She answered, "It's so lonely. Daddy and I were married for almost 70 years and he's not here." First I hugged her and

243

assured her of my love, then I replied, "You taught me to trust that God is always with us, and we were promised, 'My grace is sufficient for you'" She smiled again with that ever present smile and said, assuredly, "I have found it so!" Always thankful, no matter the circumstances, and always a presence and an influence in my life!

You understand what I mean, then, when I say, "I am grateful that I am able to be grateful." Food is tastier, relationships are richer, and all of life is so much better when you are able to approach it all with a grateful heart.

But, if we are grateful, the question remains, "How can I say thanks?" How can we give expression to our gratitude? One way is by passing on to others the good gifts we have received from God. That is one of the most important Biblical principles: We are not blessed by God so that we can indulge ourselves. No, we are blessed by God so that we can be a blessing to others. As Jesus said, "To whom much is given, much will be required." (Luke 12:48) It's a kind of spiritual tag. We are "tagged" or blessed by God and we are "it." We are then to "tag" others by blessing them as we have been blessed.

Robert Newell tells about a man who was driving down a country road just after a rain. His car went into a slide and ran into the ditch. He couldn't get out under his own power, but soon a second motorist came along, saw his predicament, and stopped to help. He backed his car up to the ditch, opened his trunk, and removed a length of strong rope. Tying it to the first man's car, he affixed the other end to his car. Then he got into his car and pulled the stuck car from the ditch. Of course the relieved driver spoke his thanks, but he felt that he should do more. He offered payment, but the good Samaritan refused. When the helped man insisted that he repay his benefactor in some way, the man said, "Okay, if you really

244

want to express your thanks, buy a strong rope and always carry it in your trunk."

That's a powerful way to express gratitude, by passing it on. If we know we are loved, then we are to love. If we know we have been forgiven, then we are to forgive. If we know that we have been given to, then we are to give. If we know that we have been blessed, then we are to be a blessing to others.

While it is essential to live out our gratitude, it is also important to verbalize our gratitude. One way of saying thanks is just to say, "Thanks." Thanksgiving Day is one of my favorite days in the year. It's family time, time to talk and just enjoy being together. Family is one of God's greatest gifts! When our family sits down to enjoy a Thanksgiving meal, we join hands around the table and say our thanks. In the midst of the love and the laughter and the feasting, we take time out to acknowledge the source of it all. And I'm just as sure of this as I am sure of anything: After saying thanks, the food always tastes better and the love always feels better.

It's good to say, "Thanks." And not just on Thanksgiving Day. Once we develop a thanksgiving approach to life, we will begin to look for things to be grateful for, and we will begin to feel gratitude and to say, "Thanks" throughout every day. That's not a bad prayer, you know. As Meister Eckhart once said, "If the only prayer you say in your whole life is 'Thank you,' that would suffice."

It happened a number of years ago now, but I will never forget it. Five or six thousand Christians gathered in Fort Worth, Texas, for a time of worship. We had been invited there for what was to become one of the most exhilarating experiences of my life. At the opening service of worship, Bishop Woodie White preached the sermon. Woodie was a black Bishop from Illinois, and during the sermon he told of a visit he had made to Africa, one of the fastest growing Christian areas of the world. He told of the joy and the excitement that characterizes their Christian experience. The church there is vital and alive! Bishop White visited Zimbabwe, where he was to speak to a gathering of Christian women who met together every Friday. They walked to their meetings, all wearing uniforms, signifying their commitment and their oneness. The Bishop described his excitement as he watched the women, from all over Zimbabwe, dressed in their all white uniforms, going to their gathering. As they walked, they would sing, and that day they sang for Bishop White. A simple, but beautiful song, it took hold of his heart and would not let go. The women sang it for him first in English and then in Shona. This is their song:

> "Thank you Father, Amen. Thank you Father, Amen.
> Thank you Father, Amen.
> Hallelujah, Amen."

That's a good song for us to sing throughout the day. Just think of the gift of life and the beauty of this delightful world. Think of the rich diversity of God's gifts to you. Think of the many things God has placed here for our enjoyment, and specifically, of those special things that make life especially good for you, you know, those things that bring a smile to your face and a delight to your heart. Think of all of that and you will want to sing, "Thank you Father, Amen."

Think about the relationships of life: family and friends, special people to love and to be loved by. What a gift! It makes us want to sing, "Thank you Father, Amen."

Think about God, about all that God has done for us. In spite of our unworthiness, God has never abandoned us or forsaken us. God is always with us and God's grace is

246

sufficient for our every need. Out of his great love, God sent Jesus to us to redeem us and to bring us home to him. When I think of what Jesus has done for me, and when I think about where I might be without him, I just have to sing, "Thank you Father, Amen. Thank you Father, Amen. Thank you Father, Amen. Hallelujah, Amen."

Prayer: Thank you Father, for your love and for the many generous expressions of your love. Thank you for the privilege of expressing our thanks by the way we live, by having a part in all the loving things you are doing, and simply by saying, "Thank you, Father!" Amen.

Made in the
USA
Middletown, DE

73440400R00137